Contents

CW01501187

1

Planning Ahead for Retirement

Retirement today is a time of opportunity. Planning ahead helps to make the most of it.

Thanks to increasing life expectancy, a great many people can realistically look forward to enjoying 25 years, or longer, after leaving work. So to be prudent, planning should include your eighties (or even nineties) as well as your sixties.

This book is not designed to offer a blueprint. Its sole aim is to highlight some of the many choices, to advise on the best sources of information and to help you avoid the pitfalls that can trap the unwary.

Key concerns are likely to be the question of money and how you will occupy your time. Others may well include: where you live, how best to keep fit, the effect of your retirement on close relationships and perhaps new responsibilities such as the care of elderly parents.

You do not need to be an accountant to know that once you stop earning your income will drop. However, if you complete the Budget Planner (see page 12), you may well find that the difference is far less than you had feared. On the plus side, you will be saving on travel and other work-related expenses as well as enjoying a welcome reduction in tax.

You may also have savings: a lump sum from your pension and perhaps insurance policies. If so, it would be wise to draw up a plan for maximising their value. Should you invest your money in a building society, ISA, unit trust or other outlet? Does it make sense to buy an annuity? What are the tax angles? If you are unsure of some of the answers, then the investment tips in Chapter 5 may help.

Your income may well depend on whether you get a new job. We are not pretending this is easy, but a great many men and women do in fact find rewarding work when they are well into their sixties.

A worthwhile alternative could be to devote your energies to voluntary work. There are scores of opportunities for retired people to make a valuable contribution within their own community. Whether you can only spare the occasional day or help on a regular basis, you will find lots of ideas in Chapter 9.

A prime requirement, whether you are thinking of paid or unpaid work, or for that matter simply planning to devote more time to your hobbies, is to remain fit and healthy. While anyone can be unfortunate enough to be struck down by an illness, the reason why the seventies are so often dogged by aches and pains is that sufficient care has not been taken in earlier years.

As well as all the obvious advice about not smoking or drinking to excess, there is the important question of exercise. While you could do press-ups and go for walks, you will probably have a much better time if you join the new keep-fit brigade. There are opportunities today for almost every kind of sport, with 50-plus beginners especially welcome. Additionally dancing, yoga and keep-fit classes are available through most local authorities.

The only problem is likely to be fitting everything in. The choice of leisure pursuits is little short of staggering. If you have ever wanted to learn about computers, take a degree, join a choir, become proficient in a craft or know more about wildlife, you will find an organisation that caters for your interest.

The type of activities you enjoy could be an important consideration in choosing where you will live. Because we tend to think of retirement as a time for moving home, many people up sticks without perhaps giving enough thought to such essentials as proximity to family and friends and whether a new area would provide the same scope for pursuing their interests.

While moving may be the right solution, especially if you want to realise some capital, there are plenty of ways of adapting a home to make it more convenient and labour-saving. You may also be able to cut the running costs, for example with insulation. These and other possibilities, including creating a granny flat, are explored in Chapter 7.

On the subject of granny flats, if you are caring for elderly parents there may come a time when a little outside help could make all the difference. The range of organisations that can provide you with back-up is far more extensive than is generally realised. While there may be pressure if a parent, however much loved, requires an undue amount of attention, a more commonplace problem is the effect of retirement on a couple's relationship.

Many husbands are puzzled, and sometimes hurt, by their wife's attitude. For years she has been complaining 'I never see anything of you darling' – so naturally he expects her to be delighted to have him at home. But according to some husbands, the enthusiasm may seem less than whole-hearted.

Put in blunt terms, many wives grumble that having a husband at home means an extra meal to cook. And while this may not apply in marriages where couples share the domestic jobs equally, in a majority of households women still do the lion's share of the cooking and cleaning. So, if he stays in bed longer, the chores will be finished later which can be an irritation. An even greater cause for resentment is that she may feel guilty about enjoying her usual activities unless her partner is also busy.

If she is still at work, the situation can be even more fraught as she may find her loyalties uncomfortably divided. Furthermore, quite irrationally, some retired husbands begin to imagine office romances that had never crossed their mind before.

Sometimes too, retired people subconsciously label themselves as 'old' and start denying themselves and their partner the pleasures of a happy sex life. It is difficult to know whether this is more ludicrous or tragic. As research shows, the sexual satisfaction of both partners continues in very many cases long after the age of seventy and often well into the eighties.

Usually, problems that coincide with retirement can be fairly simply overcome by willingness to discuss them and to work out a solution that suits both partners.

Many non-marrieds also face tricky adjustments. Relatives may impose new pressures once you leave work. Close friendships sometimes alter when one friend retires – and not the other. Also, many people admit that they had not realised before how much they relied on their job for companionship.

Pre-retirement courses

Talking to other people can be immensely helpful. If you have not been lucky enough to attend a pre-retirement course but would be interested, the following organisations should be able to advise you.

The Pre-Retirement Association of Great Britain & Northern Ireland, 9 Chesham Road, Guildford, Surrey GU1 3LS. T:01483 301170. The PRA runs two-day retirement planning courses in Central London, Slough, Guildford, Reigate and Leeds. Price is £255 per person, or £405 per couple (excluding VAT). Some local organisations affiliated to the PRA also run courses, details from the above address.

The Retirement Trust, 19 Borough High Street, London SE1 9SE. T:020 7378 9708. Runs pre-retirement seminars, lasting a day, once a month in Central London. Price, including lunch, is £125 or £200 per couple.

Scottish Pre-Retirement Council, Alexandra House, 204 Bath Street, Glasgow G2 4HL. T:0141 332 9427. Runs courses in various parts of Scotland. These are normally held over three days and cost about £60.

Adult education centres. For information about local courses, see telephone directory under your local council listing.

Workers' Educational Association, Temple House, 17 Victoria Park Square, Bethnal Green, London E2 9PB. T:020 8983 1515. Many WEA branches run local courses. Contact branch office or the London HQ for information.

New focus for the retired

A number of organisations have been formed to represent the interests of retired people and to give them a more powerful voice in putting forward their views on issues that affect their lives. Three of the best known are:

Age Resource, 1268 London Road, Norbury, London SW16 4ER. T:020 8765 7610. Promotes positive ageing by proving that over-50s are not just capable of leading fulfilling lives but that they also have a positive contribution to make. Among other activities, it runs an award scheme for projects involving significant numbers of mature people and operates a nationwide network of Age Resource Desks that offer Internet and e-mail taster sessions together with information about local opportunities for leisure, voluntary work and further learning.

ARP/O5, Greencoat House, Francis Street, London SW1P 1DZ. T:020 7828 0500. Among other facilities, there are three free emergency helplines (legal, tax and domestic), a magazine and various social events. Membership costs £24 a year (£31 per couple) by direct debit.

National Pensioners Convention, 47 Chalton Street, London NW1 1HY. T:020 7388 9807. The NPC is an umbrella group for pensioner associations throughout the country. Among other activities, a main aim is to act as a pressure group to improve facilities and opportunities for older people. For further information and addresses of local groups, contact the NPC at the above address.

2

Money Matters

For most people approaching retirement, the major concern is money. The fact that most of their friends who have already retired seem to manage pretty well is of little comfort. Even quite wealthy individuals confess to conjuring up images of going cold and hungry.

Happily, the reality is far rosier than many people imagine. The dread of drastic economies that haunts so many men and women is often due to their having only the haziest idea as to their likely income and expenditure.

Doing the sums

Knowing the facts is the first priority. To make a proper assessment, you need to draw up several lists:

- Expected sources of income on retirement
- Unavoidable outgoings
- Normal additional spending (including holidays).

Stage two, you need to consider options under the following headings:

- Possible ways of boosting your retirement income
- Spending now for saving later
- Cherished plans, if affordable.

Most difficult of all, you will require a third list of variables and unknowns which, while impossible to estimate accurately, must be taken into account in any long-term budget planning. The two most important are tax and inflation. Also, there are all the possible emergency situations such as your health for which, if this ever were to become a problem, you might want to make special provision. Your life expectancy is another consideration, as is that of your partner.

Ideally, you should start thinking about at least some of these points, especially those that relate to your pension, five or even ten years before you retire. When doing the sums, aim to be realistic. Many people make the mistake of basing their calculations on their current expenditure, without realising that some of their needs will change. It is a good idea to imagine yourself already retired. The good news is that, while some items will probably eat more of your budget, others will certainly be cheaper or no longer cost you anything at all.

Possible savings and extra outgoings are discussed below. The most practical way of examining the list is to tick off the items that you expect definitely to apply and, where possible, to write down the expenditure involved. See Budget Planner, pages 12–16.

Possible savings

When you leave your job, you will probably save at least several pounds a week. Items for which you will no longer have to pay include: your travel costs to work, bought lunches, special clothes; plus all the incidentals such as drinks with colleagues and collections for the Christmas party.

You will not have to pay any more NI contributions and, unless you choose to invest in a private plan, your pension payments will also cease. Additionally, when you retire, you may be in a lower tax bracket.

At the same time you may have reached the stage when your children are now independent, your mortgage is substantially paid off and you have stopped subscribing to a life assurance policy. Moreover, one of the advantages of reaching state pension age (or sometimes 60 for both sexes) is that you become eligible for a variety of benefits, e.g.: concessionary travel, free NHS prescriptions, cheaper theatre tickets (usually matinees) and a wide choice of special holiday offers. Also, many insurance companies give discounts to mature drivers. The normal qualifying age is 50 to 55. Some also offer retired householders' insurance policies at substantially reduced rates.

Extra outgoings

There is no escaping the fact that when you retire some of your expenses will be heavier than at present.

Firstly, you will probably be spending more time at home, so items like heating and lighting are liable to be costlier.

If you received any perks with your job, such as a company car or health insurance, then these will have to come out of your own pocket in future. Any free business lunches will also cease.

Another important consideration is your extra leisure. With more time available, you will understandably be tempted to spend more on outings, hobbies and on longer holidays from home. To avoid having to stint yourself, these need to be budgeted for in advance. Even voluntary activity is not without its hidden expenses, for example: more use of the telephone, petrol costs, raffle tickets and so on.

Looking ahead, as you get older you may want more home comforts. Likewise, you may have to pay other people to do some of the jobs, such as the decorating, that you previously managed yourself.

Anticipating the areas of extra expenditure is not to be pessimistic. On the contrary, it is the surest way of avoiding future money worries.

Expected sources of income on retirement

Your list will include at least some of the following. Once you have added up the figures in the budget planner, you will have to deduct income tax to arrive at the net spending amount available to you.

- State basic pension
- Occupational pension
- State graduated pension
- Personal pension
- SERPS
- State benefits

You may receive money from some of the following:

- Company share option scheme
- National Savings interest
- Endowment policy
- Other existing income (from a trust, property, family business)
- Investments (stocks and shares, building society etc.)
- Sale of business or personal assets
- Bank deposit account

Unavoidable outgoings

One person's priority is another person's luxury – and vice versa. For this reason, the divide between 'unavoidable' and 'normal additional spending' (see section following) is fraught with obvious difficulty. For example, readers who do not possess a pet would never include pet food among the essentials, whereas a dog or cat owner unquestionably would.

Almost everyone will want to juggle some of the items between the two lists; or add extra outgoings omitted by us. What matters is the basic principle behind the exercise. If at some stage budgeting choices have to be made, decisions will be easier if you already know: your total outgoings, what you are spending on each and those you variously rate as important or marginal.

Whatever your own essentials, some of the following items will certainly feature on your list of unavoidable expenses:

- Food
- Rent or mortgage repayments
- Council tax
- Repair and maintenance costs
- Heating
- Lighting and other energy
- Telephone
- TV licence/rental
- Household insurance
- Clothes
- Domestic cleaning products
- Laundry, cleaners' bills, shoe repair
- Miscellaneous services, e.g plumber, window cleaner
- Car, including licence, petrol, AA, etc.
- Other transport
- Regular savings and life assurance
- HP/other loan repayments
- Outgoings on health

Normal additional expenditure

This may well include:

- Gifts
- Holidays
- Newspapers/books
- Drink
- Cigarettes/tobacco
- Hairdressing
- Toiletries/cosmetics
- Expenditure on pets
- Entertainment (hobbies, outings, videos, home entertaining etc.)
- Misc. subscriptions/ membership fees
- Charitable donations
- Other

Work out the figures against these lists. Then in order to compare your expenditure against likely income, jot them down on the Budget Planner.

Possible ways of boosting your retirement income

Other than luck, there are three main possibilities for providing you with extra money: your home, work and investment skill.

Your home

Your home offers several different options.

Moving somewhere smaller. You could sell your present home, move into smaller accommodation and end up with the double bonus of pocketing a lump sum and reducing your running costs.

The cash difference on the exchange will almost certainly be less than you hope. What with removal charges and lawyers' fees, moving home is a very expensive business. You may also have some decorating expenses and there is bound to be a short overlap when you will be paying two lots of telephone rental, extra electricity bills and so on. This is not to say that moving may not be an excellent decision; simply that, if money is the main criterion, you need to be thoroughly realistic when calculating the gains.

Ideally, you should try to dovetail selling and buying at the same time. If this is not possible (and it usually isn't), the golden advice must be to sell first rather than risk lumbering yourself with the expense of a bridging loan.

Taking in lodgers. If you have more space than you need, you could consider taking in lodgers, either as paying guests or, if your property lends itself to the creation of a separate flatlet, in a tenancy capacity.

You are allowed to receive up to £4,250 a year free of tax. **Tax relief only applies to accommodation that is 'part of your main home', so if you are thinking of creating a separate flatlet, you will need to take care that this qualifies and is not at risk of being assessed as a commercial let.** Check with your architect or other professional adviser that he/she fully understands the technical requirements.

Raising money on your home. You could part-sell your home either for a capital sum or regular payments, under an equity-release scheme, and continue to live in it for as long as you wish. Sounds wonderful? There are both attractions and drawbacks. A solicitor's advice is essential.

Work

If you want to continue working, you might be able to stay in your present job and defer your pension. See 'Ways to increase your pension', page 21.

Alternatively, you may see retirement as the opportunity for a job switch or the chance to set up on your own. When assessing your budget plans, it is as well not to count on a splendid salary as – although this is improving – many 'retirement jobs' are notoriously badly paid.

If you are thinking of becoming self-employed or starting a business, you will not only have start-up costs but few new enterprises are immediately profitable.

On the other hand, while you are working you will not be spending money on entertainment. There may also be tax advantages and scope for improving your pension. Lastly, you may be one of the lucky ones for whom work after retirement really pays.

Investment

You do not need to be very rich, nor under 60, to start thinking about investing.

Investment can take many forms, with something to suit almost everyone. We do suggest that you at least look at Chapter 5, since maximising your income in retirement could make all the difference to your enjoyment of life.

Spending now for saving later

Although you may think that there is never a best time for spending, retirement planning is different in that sooner or later you will need, or want, to make certain purchases – or pay off outstanding commitments, such as a mortgage. Most people's priority list includes one or more of the following:

- Expenditure on their home
- The purchase of a car
- The termination of HP or other credit arrangement.

There may also be a number of purchases which you had been promising yourself for some time, with the only question being 'deciding when'. To help you assess whether a policy of 'spending now' is sensible, or possibly self-indulgent, there are two very simple questions you should ask:

- Can I afford it more easily now – or in the future?
- By paying now rather than waiting, shall I be saving money in the long run?

True, the issue may be more complicated but for most choices this very basic analysis helps greatly to clarify the financial arguments on both sides.

Home improvements. If you plan to stay where you are, at some point you will probably want to make some changes or improvements: install central heating, insulate the loft, modernise the kitchen or perhaps create an extra bathroom.

Some people find it easier, and more reassuring, to pay major household bills while they are still earning. Others specifically plan to use part of the lump sum from their pension to create a dream home.

To find the answer that makes best financial sense, present commitments have to be weighed against likely future expenditure (together with what money you will have available). Equally, as with insulation, you will need to work out what long term savings you could enjoy by taking the plunge now. There is also the safety aspect: if you have bad lighting or dangerously worn carpet on part of the staircase, waiting a few years could prove very false economy.

Another important question is how certain you are that you intend to stay in your present home. Investing a fortune and then moving a couple of years later is generally a recipe for being out of pocket.

Purchasing a car. There could be two good reasons for buying a new car before you retire. One is that you have a company car that you are about to lose. The other is that your existing vehicle is beginning (or will probably soon start) to give you trouble. If either of these apply, it probably makes sense to buy a replacement while you are still feeling relatively flush.

Paying off HP and similar. In general, this is a good idea since delay is unlikely to save you any money – and may actually cost you more. The only precaution is to check the small print of your agreement, to ensure that there is no penalty for early repayment.

A further exception could be your mortgage as, although mortgage interest relief has now been abolished, there might nevertheless be some advantage in keeping one. An accountant would advise you.

Extra income

There are a great many state benefits designed to give special help to people in need. This applies, among others, to problems connected with: health, housing, care of a disabled relative, widowhood and problems encountered by the frail elderly.

While many of these benefits are 'means-tested', i.e. are only given to people whose income is below a certain level, some, such as disability living allowance, do not depend on how poor or wealthy you are. Even when 'means-testing' is a factor, income levels are often nothing like as low as many people imagine. Because this is not widely enough known, many people are not claiming help to which they are entitled. In particular, it is estimated that nearly a million pensioners are not claiming Minimum Income Guarantee (see page 22).

The main benefits and allowances are listed in their appropriate chapters, for example, Housing Benefit appears in the 'Home Decisions' chapter; invalid care allowance is briefly described in the chapter 'When Parents Need Extra Help'.

Unclaimed money owing to you

Many people lose track of their financial assets, either because they have forgotten about them or because they do not know how to contact the relevant organisation that owes them money. If you think this could apply to you, the Unclaimed Assets Register might be able to help. The products they cover include: life policies, personal and occupational pensions, unit trusts and dividends. There is a small search fee, ranging from £15 to £25, which is payable whether or not they are successful. For further information, contact the **Unclaimed Assets Register Ltd.**, Lloyds Chambers, 1 Portsoken Street, London E1 8DF. T:0870 241 1713.

Budget planner

Whether you are about to retire tomorrow or not for several years, completing the following Budget Planner (even if there are a great many gaps) is well worth the effort.

An imaginative tip, given to us by one of the retirement magazines, is to start living on your retirement income some six months before you retire. Not only will you see if your budget estimates are broadly correct but since most people err on the cautious side when they first retire, you will have the added bonus of all the extra money you will have saved.

1. Possible savings when you retire

Item   *Estimated monthly savings*

National insurance contributions   _____
Pension payments   _____
Travel expenses to work   _____
Bought lunches   _____
Incidentals at work, e.g. drinks with
   colleagues, collections for presents   _____
Special work clothes   _____
Concessionary travel   _____
Free NHS prescriptions   _____
Mature drivers' insurance policy   _____
Retired householders' insurance policy   _____
Life assurance payments and/or
possible endowment policy premiums   _____
Other   _____

TOTAL   _____

N.B. You should also take into account reduced running costs, if you move to a smaller home; any expenses for dependent children that may cease; plus other costs, e.g. mortgage payments, that may end around the time you retire. Also the fact that you may be in a lower tax bracket.

2. Possible extra outgoings when you retire

Items   *Estimated monthly cost*

Extra heating/lighting bills   _____
Extra spending on hobbies and other entertainment   _____
Longer, or more frequent, holidays   _____
Replacement of company car   _____
Private health care insurance   _____
Life/permanent health insurance   _____
Cost of substituting other perks, e.g. expense
   account lunches   _____
Out-of-pocket expenses for voluntary work activity   _____
Other   _____

TOTAL   _____

N.B. Looking ahead, you will need to make provision for any extra home comforts you might want; and also, at some point, of having to pay other people to do some of the jobs that you normally manage yourself. If you intend to make regular donations to a charity, this too should be included on the list. The same applies to any new private pension or savings plan that you might want to invest in to boost your long term retirement income.

Note on Table 3
Many people have difficulty understanding the tax system and you should certainly take professional advice if you are in any doubt at all.

However, if you fill in the following table carefully, it should give you a pretty good idea of your income after retirement and enable you to make at least provisional plans.

Remember too that you may have one or two capital sums to invest, such as:

- the commuted lump sum from your pension
- money from an endowment policy
- gains from the sale of company shares (SAYE or other share option scheme)
- profits from the sale of your home or other asset
- windfall profits from a building society
- money from an inheritance

3. Expected sources of income on retirement

A. *Income Received Before Tax* _____
   State basic pension _____
   Graduated pension _____
   SERPS _____
   Occupational pension(s) _____
   Self-employed or personal pension _____
   State benefits _____
   Investments and savings plans paid gross
     (gilts, National Savings) _____
   Casual or other pre-tax earnings _____
   Total _____
   Less Personal Tax Allowance and
     possibly also Married Couple's Allowance _____
   The 10 per cent rate tax on the first
     £1,880 of taxable income _____
   Basic Rate Tax _____
   TOTAL A _____

B. *Income Received After Tax* _____
    Dividends (unit trusts, shares, etc.) _____
    Bank deposit account _____
    Building society interest _____
    Annuity income _____
    Other (incl. earnings subject to PAYE) _____
    TOTAL B _____

TOTAL A + TOTAL B _____

    Less   Higher rate tax (if any) _____
    Plus   Other tax-free receipts, e.g. some
             State benefits, income from a matured
             TESSA, PEP plan, ISA _____
    Investment Bond withdrawals etc. _____
    Other _____

TOTAL NET INCOME _____

4. Unavoidable outgoings

Items	*Estimated monthly cost*
Food	_____
Rent or mortgage repayments	_____
Council tax	_____
Repair and maintenance costs	_____
Heating	_____
Lighting and other energy	_____
Telephone	_____
TV licence/rental	_____
Postage (incl. Christmas cards)	_____
Household insurance	_____
Clothes	_____
Laundry, cleaner's bills, shoe repair	_____
Domestic cleaning products	_____
Misc. services, e.g. plumber, window cleaner	_____
Car (incl. licence, petrol etc.)	_____
Other transport	_____
Regular savings/life assurance	_____
HP/other loan repayments	_____
Outgoings on health	_____
Other	_____
TOTAL (see over)	_____

N.B. Before adding up the total, you should look at the 'Normal Additional Expenditure' list, as you may well want to juggle some of the items between the two.

5. Normal additional expenditure

Items	*Estimated monthly cost*
Gifts	
Holidays	_____
Newspapers/books/videos	_____
Drink	_____
Cigarettes/tobacco	_____
Hairdressing	_____
Toiletries/cosmetics	_____
Entertainment (hobbies, outings, home entertaining etc.)	_____
Misc. subscriptions/membership fees	_____
Charitable donations	_____
Expenditure on pets	_____
Other	_____
TOTAL	_____

N.B. For some items, such as holidays and gifts, you may tend to think in annual expenditure terms. However, for the purpose of comparing monthly income versus outgoings, it is probably easier if you itemise all the expenditure in the same fashion. Moreover, if you need to save for a special event such as your holiday, it helps if you get into the habit of putting so much aside every month (or even weekly).

3

Understanding Your Pension

Next to your home, your pension is almost certainly your most valuable asset. It is therefore important to check all the angles well ahead of time to ensure that when you retire you receive the maximum benefit.

State pensions

You can get a pension if you are a man of 65 or a woman of 60, provided you have paid (or been credited with) sufficient national insurance contributions.

If you are an employee, your employer will have automatically deducted Class 1 contributions from your salary, provided your earnings were above a certain limit (currently £87 a week).

If you are self-employed you will have been paying a flat-rate Class 2 contribution every week and possibly the earnings-related Class 4 contributions as well.

You may also have paid Class 3 voluntary contributions at some point in your life in order to maintain your contributions record.

If you are over pension age (65 for men and 60 for women) you do not need to pay national insurance contributions.

If you have not paid sufficient NI contributions to qualify for a full rate basic pension you may be entitled to a reduced rate of pension. However, your NI contributions record will have been maintained in the following circumstances:

If you have lived or worked outside Great Britain. If you have lived in Northern Ireland or the Isle of Man, any contributions paid there will count towards your pension.

The same should also apply in most cases if you have lived or worked in a European Union country or any country whose social security system is linked to Britain's by a reciprocal agreement. Your local Social Security office will be able to advise you.

If you have received Home Responsibilities Protection (HRP). This would be likely to apply if, since 1978, you had to give up work for some time to care for a child or for a sick, or elderly, person. See page 42.

If you have been in any of the following situations, you will have been credited with contributions (instead of having to pay them):

- If you were sick or unemployed (provided you sent in sick notes to your Social Security office, signed on at the Unemployment Benefit office or had been in receipt of jobseeker's allowance);
- If you were a man aged 60–64 and not working;
- If you were entitled to maternity allowance, invalid care allowance or unemployability supplement;
- If you were taking an approved course of training;
- When you left education but had not yet started working.

Married women and widows who do not qualify for a basic pension in their own right may be entitled to some pension on their husband's contributions (see 'Pensions for Women' at the end of the chapter).

Reduced rate contributions note. Many women retiring today may have paid a reduced rate contribution at some time. Sadly this does not count towards your pension.

If you are still some years away from retirement, it could be to your advantage to cancel the reduced rate option, as by doing so you may be able to build up a wider range of benefits without paying anything extra. For advice, contact your local tax office.

How your pension is worked out

Anyone wanting to work out what they are due can ask for a 'pension forecast'. For details on how to apply, see Form BR 19, obtainable from any Social Security office.

It is worth getting an early forecast as it may be possible to improve your NI contribution record by making additional Class 3 voluntary contributions. These can only be paid for six years in arrears, so this concession may not help if you think about it too late.

Your total pension can come from three main sources: the basic pension, the additional pension and the graduated pension.

Basic pension

The full basic pension for a man or woman (April 2001/02) is £72.50 a week, £115.90 for a married couple (unless your spouse is entitled to more than the £43.40 spouse's addition on his/her own contributions, in which case you will receive more).

All pensions are taxable other than one or two special categories, such as war widows. If, however, your basic pension is your only source of income, you will not have to worry about income tax.

The rate of basic pension depends on your record of NI contributions over your working life. To get the full rate you must have paid (or been credited with) NI contributions for roughly nine-tenths of your working life, although widows can also be entitled to a full basic pension on their husband's contributions. If you are divorced, you may be able to use your former spouse's contributions to improve your own pension entitlement, provided that you have not remarried before reaching pension age.

Your working life, for this purpose, is normally considered to be 44 years for a woman and 49 years for a man (i.e. age 16 until pension age), but it may be less if you were of working age but not in insurable employment when the National Insurance Scheme started in 1948.

Reduced rate pension

If you do not have full contributions but have maintained your contributions record for between a quarter and nine-tenths of your working life, you may get a pension at a reduced rate.

Additional pension

This is also known as SERPS, short for the State Earnings Related Pension Scheme. It is worked out on earnings since April 1978 on which you have paid Class 1 contributions as an employee. It is not applicable to the self-employed.

Class 1 contributions are paid as a percentage of earnings, currently between £87 and £575 a week.

How much additional pension you get depends on the amount of your earnings over and above the lower earnings limit for each complete tax year since April 1978. The current maximum to which you could be entitled is £131.35 a week. Full details and examples of how the additional pension is worked out can be found in leaflet NP 46 *A Guide to Retirement Pensions*.

As you probably know, if you think you can do better by making independent provision, you are not obliged to remain in SERPS. For details, see 'Personal Pensions' further in the chapter.

If you are a member of a contracted-out occupational pension scheme, you are legally entitled either to a pension which must be broadly the same, or better, than you would have got under the State scheme; or to what are known as protected rights (i.e. your and your employer's compulsory contributions to your pension together with their accumulated investment growth).

Important changes to SERPS

Two important changes affecting SERPS are in the pipeline.

Firstly, as you may already know, SERPS benefits paid to surviving spouses are due to be halved over the coming years. However, contrary to the government's earlier plans, the cut is not happening in one fell swoop but instead is being gradually phased in between October 2002 and October 2010. Additionally, anyone over State pension age before 6 October 2002 will be exempt from any cuts and will keep the right to pass on their SERPS pension in full to a bereaved spouse, regardless of how many years away this may be. Equally, any younger widow or widower who had already inherited their late spouse's SERPS entitlement before 6 October 2002 will not be affected and will continue to receive the full amount. The DSS table below shows how the cuts apply to those reaching State pension age between October 2002 and 2010. If you have any queries, call the helpline on T:0845 600 6116; textphone: 0845 6012 1913.

% SERPS passing to surviving spouse	Date when contributor reaches State pension age
100%	5.10.2002 or earlier
90%	6.10.2002 – 5.10.2004
80%	6.10.2004 – 5.10.2006
70%	6.10.2006 – 5.10.2008
60%	6.10.2008 – 5.10.2010
50%	6.10.2010 or later

Rather more fundamental, the government has announced plans to discontinue SERPS and to replace it with two new schemes: the Stakeholder Pension which was launched in April 2001 and the Second State Pension (SSP) which is due to be introduced in April 2002.

Graduated pension

This pension existed between April 1961 and April 1975. The amount you receive depends on the graduated NI contributions you paid during that period. Anyone over 18 and earning more than £9 a week at that time will probably be entitled to a small graduated pension. This includes married women and widows with reduced contribution liability. A widow or widower whose spouse dies when they are both over pension age can inherit half of the graduated pension based on their late spouse's contributions.

Second State Pension and Stakeholder Pensions

As mentioned above, the government is planning to discontinue SERPS and to replace it with the existing Stakeholder Pension and a new Second State Pension.

Those contracted into SERPS will not suffer any loss, as they will still keep the benefit of any contributions made. Equally of course, those already in receipt of the additional pension (i.e. SERPS) will continue to receive their payments as normal.

Although some of the detail is still awaited, a major aim of the reforms is to help individuals who are not in a company pension scheme and whose earnings are less than £20,000 build up a better pension for the future.

It is also intended that all adults should receive an annual statement, showing them how much private and State pension they are likely to get on retirement.

Second State Pension (SSP). The main beneficiaries will be: (1) people earning less than £9,000 who will be able to save towards a very much better pension and (2) carers and others who qualify for Home Responsibilities Protection – plus also people who because of a disability have a broken work record – who will receive credits equivalent to their earning £9,000.

Stakeholder Pensions were launched on 6 April 2001. They are likely to be of most interest to those earning between £10,000 and £20,000 but are available to anyone except individuals in final salary schemes whose earnings are over £30,000. As stakeholder pensions are very similar to personal pensions, it seems more helpful to describe them in the same part of the chapter. For further information, see page xx.

Ways to increase your pension

Deferring your pension. Your pension may be increased if you delay claiming it and instead continue working after normal retirement age. For every year that you defer retirement, approximately another 7.5 per cent will be added to your pension. This extra pension is paid either when you claim your pension or when you reach 70 (65 for women), regardless of whether you have retired from work or not.

An exception to the age rule sometimes applies in the case of a married woman over 65 whose pension is based on her husband's contributions. Her pension can continue to increase until such time as her husband gets his pension or reaches the age of 70, whichever is sooner.

Warning. If you plan to defer your pension, you should also defer any graduated pension to which you may be entitled – or you risk losing the increases you would otherwise obtain.

Increases for dependants. Your basic pension may be increased if you are supporting a dependent spouse or children. Most typically, this applies in respect of a non-working wife (or one whose earnings are very low) who is under 60 when her husband retires. It also applies for a retired wife supporting a husband dependent by reason of invalidity. For further information, see BA leaflet GL23 *Social Security Benefit Rates*, obtainable from any Social Security office.

Age addition. Your pension will be automatically increased once you reach 80. The current rate is 25p a week.

Income support

If you have an inadequate income, you may qualify for Income Support. There are special premiums (i.e. additions) for lone parents, disabled people, carers and pensioners.

A condition of entitlement is that you should not have capital, including savings, of more than £8,000. To qualify for maximum income support, the capital limit is £3,000. For every £250 of capital over £3,000, individuals are deemed to be getting £1 a week income – so the actual amount of benefit will be reduced accordingly.

A big advantage is that people entitled to income support receive full help with their rent and should also not have any council tax to pay. See 'Housing benefit' and 'Council tax benefit', in Chapter 7.

If your only source of income is your basic State pension, you are likely to be entitled to income support.

N.B. All pensioners are guaranteed at least a minimum income, known as **Minimum Income Guarantee (MIG)**. For single pensioners, this is £92.15 a week; for couples, the amount is £140.55. In April 2002, the rates are being increased to £100 for a single pensioner and to £154 for a couple. These totals exclude mortgage interest and disregarded income, for example, attendance allowance.

A further helpful point is that the capital limits are more generous than those applicable to standard income support. Instead of the normal £3,000 and £8,000 limits, people aged 60 and over can have capital of up to £6,000 to qualify for maximum support or up to £12,000 to be eligible for partial support.

Those not receiving their full entitlement should be contacted by a personal adviser to help ensure they receive the money. If you do not hear from a personal adviser and your income is below £12,000, contact your local Social Security office.

Social fund. If you are faced with an exceptional expense you find difficult to pay, you may be able to obtain a Budgeting or Crisis Loan, or Funeral Payment, from the Social Fund. Ask at your Social Security office.

Working after you start getting your pension

This used to be a problem for many people as a result of the Earnings Rule. At the time, men between the ages of 65 and 69 and women between the ages of 60 and 64 who earned more than £75 a week had their basic State pension reduced. Happily, this does not apply any more and today there is no longer any limit to the amount pensioners can earn.

Early retirement and your pension

Because so many people retire early, there is a widespread belief that it is possible to get an early pension. While the information is correct as regards many employers' occupational pension schemes, it does not apply to the basic State pension.

If you retire before you are 60, you may need to pay voluntary Class 3 NI contributions in order to protect your contributions record. Men over 60, however, automatically get contribution credits from the tax year in which they reach 60.

How you get a pension

You should claim your pension shortly before you reach State pension age. The Department for Work and Pensions should send you a claim form (BR 1) but if this does not arrive, then it is your responsibility to contact them. They will send the form to the last recorded address they hold for you, so if you have moved and not informed them make sure they have your new address. You should apply for the form about four months before you are due to retire. Or, if you prefer, instead of using a claim form you can ring the National Tele-Claim Service on T:0845 300 1084 and give your details over the phone.

How your pension can be paid

If you live in the UK, you can choose to have your pension paid either by credit transfer or in order book form.

Credit transfer. This method gives you the choice of having your pension paid direct into a bank or National Giro account; or, alternatively, into an investment account with either the National Savings Bank or with most building societies. Payment will be made in arrears every four weeks, or quarterly, whichever you prefer.

Order book. You receive a book of orders (or pension book) which you can cash at a post office of your choice. Each order is your pension entitlement for one week and is valid for 12 weeks after the date shown on the voucher.

Other situations. Pensions can be paid to an overseas address, if you are going abroad for six months or more. For further details see leaflets NI 38 *Social Security Abroad*, obtainable from Inland Revenue (NI Contributions) offices and GL 29 *Going Abroad and Social Security Benefits*, obtainable from any Social Security office. If you are planning to retire abroad and have any queries about your pension, contact the International Payments Office, Pensions and Overseas Benefits Directorate, Tyneview Park, Newcastle upon Tyne NE98 1BA. T:0191 218 7777.

If you are in hospital, your pension can still be paid to you. You will receive a reduced amount if you are in hospital for more than six weeks. BA leaflet GL12 *Going Into Hospital?* (from any Social Security office) provides full information.

Christmas bonus. This is paid with your normal pension at the start of December. The bonus is £10 and is tax free.

Advice

If you have any queries or think you may not be obtaining your full pension entitlement, contact your local Social Security office as soon as possible. If you think a mistake has been made, you have the right to appeal and can insist on your claim being heard by an independent Social Security Tribunal. Before doing so, you would be strongly advised to consult a solicitor at the Citizens' Advice Bureau or the Welfare Advice Unit of your Social Security office.

If you are writing to your Social Security office with a query you should quote either your national insurance number (or your spouse's) or your pension number if you have already started receiving your pension.

For further information about pensions, see leaflets RM1 *Retirement*, RM2 *Approaching Retirement?*, RM3 *Retired?* and booklet NP 46 *A Guide to Retirement Pensions*, obtainable from any Social Security office; and PM2 *You and State Pensions*, obtainable by calling the Pensions Info-Line on T:0845 731 3233.

Private pensions

Private pension schemes fall into two broad categories: those arranged by employers, e.g. company pension schemes, and those you can arrange for yourself. In both cases, investing in a pension scheme is one of the most tax effective ways of saving for the future.

- You get income tax relief on contributions at your highest tax rate.
- The pension fund is totally exempt from income tax and capital gains tax.
- Part of the pension can be taken as a cash sum when you retire and that too is tax free.

Company pension schemes

The basic points, which apply to all company schemes, are as follows.

Pension fund. Pension contributions go into a pension fund, run by trustees, which is quite separate from your employer's company. It is the job of the trustees to manage the fund and to ensure that the benefit promises are kept.

Payments into the fund. Your scheme may or may not ask for a contribution from you. For this reason, schemes are known as 'contributory' or 'non-contributory'. If (as is normally the case) you are required to make a contribution, this will be deducted from your pay before you receive it.

Your employer will also make contributions. In some schemes the amount is calculated as a fixed percentage of your earnings. In others the scheme actuary would estimate the amount that your employer needs to pay to ensure your (and other members') benefits in the future.

Benefits from the scheme. All pension scheme members should be given a booklet describing how the scheme works, what benefits it provides and other information including the address of the Pensions Ombudsman. You can ask to see a copy of the trust deed as well as the latest annual report and audited accounts.

The key benefits applicable to most pension schemes include:

- A pension due at whatever age is specified by the scheme, usually somewhere between 60 and 65 (although many companies offer early retirement provision)
- Death benefit paid out if you die before retirement age
- A widow/widower's pension paid for life no matter when you die.

Benefit limits. The Inland Revenue sets limits on pension benefits which members of company schemes can receive. The main ones are:

- The maximum pension you are allowed is two-thirds of your final pay (excluding State pension)
- If you die, the pension can be passed on to someone else but no one beneficiary can receive more than two-thirds
- The tax free lump sum, if you choose to take it, cannot be more than one and a half times salary.

The above figures are limited by a 'cap', currently based on £95,400 earnings a year. People earning less are not affected.

Types of scheme

Most employers' schemes are of the final salary or money purchase type. Other types that exist are average earnings and flat rate schemes.

Final salary scheme. Your pension is calculated as a proportion of your final pay. The amount you receive depends on two factors: the number of years you have worked for the organisation plus the fraction of final pay on which the scheme is based, typically 1/60th or 1/80th. So if you have worked 30 years for a company that has 1/60th pension scheme, you will receive 30/60ths of your final pay – in other words, half.

Final pay schemes can be contracted into or out of SERPS. If a scheme is contracted out of SERPS, it must provide a pension that is broadly equal to, or better than, its SERPS equivalent.

Money purchase scheme. Unlike final salary schemes, the amount of pension you receive is not based on a fixed formula but (within Inland Revenue limits) is dependent on the investment performance of the fund into which your own and your employer's contributions have been paid.

Different schemes have different ways of determining how members' pension entitlements are calculated, so enquire what the rules are.

An important feature of money purchase schemes is that the bulk of the fund must be used to purchase an annuity that will provide you with a guaranteed income for life. (See 'Compulsory purchase annuities' below).

Group personal pension scheme. Employers sometimes arrange group schemes for employees wishing to build up a personal pension. They are usually more advantageous than individual personal pensions because employers often make contributions into all participants' pension fund. All personal pensions, whether group or individual, are a form of money purchase scheme.

Contracted-out mixed benefit scheme (COMBS). This is a mixed scheme, which combines elements of salary-related and money purchase schemes.

Average earnings scheme. This is based on your average earnings over the total period of time that you participate in the scheme. Every year, an amount goes into the scheme on your behalf, based on your earnings. Each year, your 'profits' are worked out from a formal table and the total of all these annual sums constitutes your pension.

Flat rate pension scheme. The same flat rate applies to everyone, multiplied by the number of years in which they have been participants of the scheme. So, for example, if the flat rate is £500 a year of pension and you have been a member of the scheme for 20 years, your pension will be £10,000 a year.

Compulsory purchase annuities

Everyone with a contracted-out company money purchase scheme (COMPS), AVC arrangement, personal pension, retirement annuity or Section 226 policy (explained on page 34), must by law purchase an annuity. Until recently, for most types of scheme, this had to be at the time of retirement. Today, however, thanks to new regulations, individuals can defer purchasing an annuity for as long as they like until age 75.

An annuity is an insurance product which guarantees an income for life. You can use the whole of your accumulated pension fund; or you can first take all, or part, of your tax free lump sum. If you take your lump sum, this will reduce the amount of annual income you receive.

You should take great care in choosing where you buy your annuity as the rates offered by life companies vary widely. Once you have made a choice, it is extremely difficult to switch.

Most people stay with their current pension provider, often because they don't realise that they have any choice. However, while 'staying put' may be the best answer, recent research shows that many people could significantly improve their pension by moving to another company for their annuity.

You can take advice from an independent financial adviser, a pensions consultant or a company that specialises in tracking annuity rates. These include: **The Annuity Bureau**, The Tower, 11 York Road, London SE1 7NX. T:020 7902 2300; **Annuity Direct**, 32 Scrutton Street, London EC2A 4RQ. T:020 7684 5000.

Annuity deferral option. As stated earlier, instead of purchasing an annuity immediately on retirement, if you wish you can now delay doing so up to the age of 75. Those who choose to wait can both take their tax-free lump sum from any age after 50 and can also withdraw a limited income during the deferral period (i.e. until they purchase an annuity). However, there can be considerable risks in withdrawing money, so expert advice is essential.

Additional voluntary contributions (AVCs)

AVCs are a very attractive way of making extra savings for retirement. Firstly, they enjoy full tax relief. They also allow you to purchase 'added years', to make up any shortfall in your entitlement to benefit under a company scheme.

You can get the same advantages with 'free-standing AVCs (FSAVCs)'. These are not linked to a company scheme but can be purchased independently from: insurance companies, building societies, banks and others. You are allowed to contribute both to company AVCs and to a free-standing plan or plans.

The total of all your AVCs plus other contributions to the pension plan is not allowed to exceed 15 per cent of your earnings. If you are already subscribing to company AVCs, check on your present level of contributions before investing in a new plan. In the event of over-funding occurring, the surplus will be refunded to you in cash, minus the tax relief involved.

For most people, the only problem with AVCs is the vast choice. You would be well advised to do some basic research into the track record of any policies you might be considering and on no account sign any document without first being absolutely certain that you fully understand all the terms and conditions.

In all cases you should be given 'key features' information, including in particular details of the charges. Also, anyone advising you about the purchase of FSAVCs must explain the basic differences between the FSAVCs being recommended and the AVCs offered by your employer's scheme. Generally speaking, the charges are likely to be lower for company AVCs than for free-standing AVCs.

Compensation for mis-sold FSAVCs. Despite the above safe-guards, there is evidence to suggest that thousands of people may have been mis-sold an FSAVC when they would have done better joining their employer's AVC scheme. A review is now under way to identify those individuals and, where appropriate, to compensate them for any financial loss.

If you were sold an FSAVC between April 1988 and 15 August 1999, you may have received a form *FSAVC Pension Top-Ups – Were You Badly Advised?* from your FSAVC firm to assess whether you should receive an invitation for a review. If you do not receive the form but believe that you would have a claim, you can request to have a review. If you want a review, you have until the end of 2002 to apply together with your reasons for doing so. Should you need advice, you can contact the FSA consumer helpline on T:0845 606 1234.

Compensation for mis-sold FSAVC is exempt from tax.

Early leavers

In recent years the government has introduced new rules which give early leavers better protection. Even so, if you are thinking of taking early retirement you should work out very carefully how this might affect your pension. Most employers apply actuarial reductions. In other words you will receive less pension than if you had stayed till normal retirement age.

An important reform concerns what are known as your **preserved rights** – in other words, your financial rights with regard to your pension. Previously you only qualified if you had been in an employer's scheme for at least five years. Today the qualifying period is two years.

There are three choices available to people with preserved rights who leave a company to switch jobs. They can leave their pension with the scheme; take it to a new employer's scheme; or take it to an insurance company.

Leaving the pension with the scheme. You will receive a pension at the scheme's normal retirement age. Your accrued pension rights will be increased by 5 per cent a year or the rate of inflation, whichever is lower. Another advantage is that you keep any existing benefits. Also, once you start receiving your pension, you would be entitled to any extra increases that may be given.

Taking your pension to a new scheme. You do not have to make an immediate decision. You can transfer your pension scheme any time, provided this is over a year before you retire.

Early leavers can move their pension – or more precisely, its transfer value – to a new employer's scheme willing to accept it. The transfer value is the cash value of your current pension rights. Calculating this can be problematic and early leavers are often at a disadvantage compared with those who remain in the scheme.

Joining a new employer's scheme does not necessarily oblige you to transfer your previous benefits. In some circumstances, there may be an argument for leaving your existing benefits with your former scheme and joining your new employer's scheme from scratch for the remaining years that you are working.

Taking your pension to an insurance company. If neither of the previous options appeal, or your new company will not accept your old pension value into its own scheme, you can go independent and have the transfer value of your pension invested by a life company into a personal scheme. After deducting its charges, the life company would invest the balance of the money in the fund, or funds, of your choice.

Advice. Deciding what's best is often very complex. Unless the issues are very clear-cut, expert advice is usually essential.

Becoming self-employed

If, as opposed to switching jobs, you leave paid employment to start your own enterprise, you are allowed to transfer your accumulated pension rights into a new fund. For most people the choice will be either to invest their money with an insurance company or to take either a personal, or stakeholder, pension.

Another possibility which might be more attractive if you are fairly close to normal retirement age is to leave your pension in your former employer's scheme. See earlier para 'Leaving the pension with the scheme'.

Minimum retirement age

At the present time, many pension schemes allow you to take early retirement and draw your pension from the age of 50. As you may have read in the press, the government is considering proposals to raise the minimum age by five years to 55. A main reason is that we are living longer and most of us have not saved enough to retire comfortably at 60, let alone younger.

The proposals envisage phasing in the change over 10 years, starting in 2010. Those born before April 1950 would not be affected.

Questions on your pension scheme

Most people find it very difficult to understand how their pension scheme works. However, your pension may be worth a lot of money and it is important that you should know the key essentials, including any options that may still be available to you.

If you have a query or are concerned about your pension, you should approach whoever is responsible for the scheme in your organisation.

The sort of questions you might ask will vary according to circumstance, such as: before you join the scheme, if you are thinking of changing jobs, if you are hoping to retire early and so on. You will probably think of plenty of additional points of your own. The questions listed are simply an indication of some of the information you may require in order to plan sensibly ahead.

Before you join the scheme

■ Ask whether the scheme is contracted in or out of SERPS and, if it is contracted in, what will happen once SERPS is abolished.

- How do you qualify to become a member? For example, there may be different conditions for different grades of staff. There may be an age ceiling for new entrants. Or a minimum period of service before you can join.
- Many companies have set up contracted-out money purchase schemes – or COMPS, as they are known for short – which operate on a different principle from final salary schemes. Ask what type of scheme you would be joining and if it is a money purchase one, how in particular members' entitlements are calculated. (See 'Money purchase scheme' page 27).
- If the scheme is a group personal pension scheme, ask what extra contributions, if any, the employer makes (3 per cent is a fairly normal figure).
- If it is a final salary scheme, is it based on 1/60th, 1/80th or other fraction?
- Another point, if it is a final salary scheme, is what guaranteed pension increases are given? Since April 1997, schemes must by law give annual increases of at least 5 per cent or the rate of inflation, whichever is lower – but some schemes are more generous.
- Are discretionary increases given in addition to the guaranteed amount?
- Is anything deducted from the scheme to allow for the State pension?
- At what age is the pension normally paid?
- Are there any extra benefits included in the scheme?

If you want to leave the organisation to change jobs

- How much will your deferred pension be worth?
- Should you wish to move the transfer value to another scheme, how long would you have to wait from the date of your request? (This should normally be within 3 to 6 months).

If you leave for other reasons

- What happens if you become ill – or die – before pension age?
- What are the arrangements if you want to retire early?

What to do before retirement

You may need to chase up any earlier schemes of which you were a member, as you could be due some extra pension.

Your previous employer/s may be able to help. If you draw a blank, best advice is to contact the Occupational Pensions Regulatory

Authority (OPRA) which manages a pensions registry and tracing service to assist people who need help in tracing their pension rights. To request a trace application form (PR4), write to: **Pension Schemes Registry**, PO Box 1NN, Newcastle upon Tyne NE99 1NN. T:0191 225 6393. This is a free service.

Other help and advice

Other sources of help to know about are: the trustees or managers of your pension scheme; OPAS; the Pensions Ombudsman.

Trustees or managers. These are the first people to contact if you do not understand your benefit entitlements or are unhappy about some other point. Ask the pensions manager for names and addresses.

OPAS, the Pensions Advisory Service. OPAS can give free help and advice, other than financial advice, on any type of pension scheme – except State pensions. If you have a specific query or just want general information, you can call the helpline on T:020 7233 8080. There is also a second helpline, specifically to do with enquiries on stakeholder pensions T:0845 601 2923. Or you can write to: **OPAS**, the Pensions Advisory Service,11 Belgrave Road, London SW1V 1RB.

Pensions Ombudsman. You would normally only approach the Ombudsman if neither the pension scheme trustees/managers nor OPAS are able to help. The Ombudsman can investigate: (1) complaints of maladministration (2) disputes of fact or law with the trustees, managers or an employer. He cannot, however, investigate: complaints about mis-selling of pension schemes, a complaint that is already subject to court proceedings or one that is about a State social security benefit.

There is no charge for the Ombudsman's service. The address to write to is: **The Pensions Ombudsman**, 11 Belgrave Road, London SW1V 1RB. T:020 7834 9144.

If you have a complaint about a personal pension, contact the **Financial Ombudsman Service**, South Quay Plaza, 183 Marsh Wall, London E14 9SR. T:0845 080 1800. It is possible that you may be referred to the Pensions Ombudsman above but if so, you will be informed very quickly.

Personal pension schemes

Everyone – whether self-employed or working for an employer – has the choice of continuing with their present pension arrangements or switching instead to a personal pension (PP) or stakeholder pension. In this section we concentrate exclusively on personal pensions. For information about stakeholder pensions, see page 39.

Although, most people over 50 are likely to be better off continuing as they are, if you are moving to a new job, are ineligible to join your company scheme or are thinking of becoming self-employed, one of the options described below may offer you an attractive solution.

Choices for the self-employed

Personal pensions are largely modelled on the old-style self-employed pensions – known as Section 226 policies.

These have now been abolished. However, anyone with an existing Section 226 policy is not affected – unless they actually wish to switch to a PP. As general wisdom, the view in the pensions industry is that for most people there would be little point in changing – and for some, it could be positively detrimental. But as with most decisions there are arguments on either side, so you should at least know what the choices are.

Differences between Section 226 policies and personal pensions. There are four main differences between Section 226 policies and PPs. These concern: the age of retirement, the method of calculating the lump sum, allowable contributions into the plan and the possible size of your pension allowed for tax relief.

- **Age of retirement**. Under a Section 226 policy, retirement cannot be taken before the age of 60. With a PP, you can retire at any time between 50 and 75.
- **Method of calculating the lump sum**. Under Section 226 contracts, this is expressed as three times the residual annuity paid. The PP rules define the amount as 25 per cent of the total fund excluding your protected rights.
- **Allowable contributions**. A Section 226 policy limits you to a maximum of 27.5 per cent of your earnings. For PPs, people over 50 can contribute up to 30 per cent, rising (depending on their age) to a maximum of 40 per cent.
- **Size of pension**. For high earners, the £95,400 cap is probably the strongest argument for hanging on to an existing Section 226 policy, since such policies are not affected by the earnings' cap.

For further information, see leaflet PM5 *Pensions for the Self-Employed*, obtainable by phoning the Pensions Info-Line on 0845 731 3233.

Personal pensions for employees

You can take a PP in place of SERPS; or alternatively, in place of your employer's scheme.

If you are a member of a good contracted-out final salary scheme – or have the opportunity of joining one – it is very unlikely that a PP would be in your best interest.

If your employer does not have a pension scheme, if you are ineligible to join or if you think you could do better for yourself than under your current scheme, then a PP could be worth considering.

A main advantage of a PP is that if you change jobs you can take it with you without penalty. There are attractive tax relief benefits. You have choice as to how your pension payments are invested and if you have built up a big enough fund, you can retire at any age between 50 and 75. Also, if you change your mind after having taken a PP, you can switch back into the State scheme; or, if the scheme rules allow it, you can transfer your payments into a company contracted-out scheme.

Alternatively, if you enter pensionable employment but do not wish to transfer your PP to your employer's scheme, you can either leave it 'frozen' or transfer it instead to an FSAVC scheme.

The big drawback of a PP, particularly for an older person, is that it may not offer you such attractive benefits as your present scheme. Most employers do not make extra contributions to a PP so, other than your rebate from SERPS or Second State Pension (SSP) when this is introduced in April 2002 (see Minimum DSS contributions below), all the investment towards your pension will need to come out of your earnings. You may also lose out on valuable benefits that are often included in an employer's scheme, e.g.: a pension before normal age were you to become ill; protection for your dependants should you die; attractive early retirement terms if you were made redundant; any increases in pension payments that the scheme may give to help offset inflation.

Before taking a decision, a first essential is to understand how PPs work.

Starting date. You can start a personal pension at any time and then, in order to receive all the DSS minimum contributions, backdate it to the start of the tax year on April 6. The formalities involved are very easy.

Contributions into your pension plan. There are three possible ways (previously four, see 'special incentive payments') of building up savings in your pension plan.

- **Minimum DSS contributions**. These will be paid into your PP automatically. They are worked out according to the level of national insurance contributions that both you and your employer are required to pay by law. The rebates vary with age: older people receive more.
- **Extra contributions made by you**. You can make extra contributions into your pension plan. If you do so, you will not only build up more savings but will have more flexibility as to when you can retire. If only the minimum DSS contributions are paid, you will have to wait until the normal State retirement age. If you make extra contributions, you can retire when you like between 50 and 75. However, see N.B. below.

There are Inland Revenue rules as to the amount you can invest, which varies according to your age. There is also a 'cap' on earnings – currently (2001/02) £95,400 – allowable for tax relief.

- If you are aged 35 or under, you can pay up to 17.5 per cent of your earnings into a personal pension.
- For ages 36 to 45: the maximum is 20 per cent.
- For ages 46 to 50: 25 per cent.
- For ages 51 to 55: 30 per cent.
- For ages 56 to 60: 35 per cent.
- If you are over 60, you can invest up to 40 per cent of your earnings.

Ages are calculated at the beginning of the tax year.

N.B. While the above age/earnings link for PP contributions normally applies, the rules were amended in April 2001 to bring the tax regime for personal pensions (and other money purchase schemes) in line with that of stakeholder pensions. The important result of this change is that as you can now make contributions of up to £3,600 a year regardless of your age or how much, or little, you earn. For further information see 'Stakeholder pensions', page 39.

- **Voluntary contributions by your employer**. Your employer might want to help you improve your pension by making extra contributions into your pension plan. Very few employers actually do so!
- **Special incentive payments**. An extra 2 per cent payment was given by the government as part of the launch of PPs. These payments have now ceased. Anyone who previously received them can look forward to enjoying the benefit when they retire.

Relating back. This is a way of varying the timing of your payments as well as maximising unused tax relief. Until recently, it also used to be possible to carry forward unused relief but sadly this option was abolished at the start of April 2001 tax year.

N.B. Higher contributions needed in future. As most people with an existing PP will be aware, as a result of a technical tax change – i.e. the abolition of ACT – anyone with a PP will need to make bigger contributions than previously to ensure a decent pension. While this will especially affect younger people, if you are still some way off retirement and haven't already done so, you should speak to your pension adviser to check what extra you should be paying to compensate for the removal of the dividend tax credit.

Your pension receipts. As with all money purchase schemes, the amount of pension you eventually receive will depend on two main factors: the size of the fund you have been able to build up and the fund's investment performance. You have a great deal of choice in the matter but there are also certain rules designed to protect you.

A basic rule concerns what are known as your **protected rights**. These are the DSS minimum contributions (including the value of the extra 2 per cent introductory payment) and tax relief you may have received – together with their accumulated investment growth.

Your protected rights can only be invested in a single contract and must be used to purchase the annuity which will pay for your annual pension when you retire. They cannot be used as a contribution towards your lump sum.

Your lump sum derives from the extra contributions that you – and perhaps also your employer – have made. You can take up to 25 per cent of this part of the fund. The remainder will be added to your protected rights to purchase a better annuity.

Choosing a pension plan. PPs are offered by insurance companies, banks, building societies, unit trusts, friendly societies and independent financial advisers (IFAs). Before deciding, you should aim to look at a variety of plans (see 'Types of investment policy' below). Also ask any questions about points that are unclear or technical terms that you do not fully understand – including in particular any questions you may have about the charges.

The law now requires anyone selling PPs to state their charges (including commission) in writing. Advisers must also put in writing their reasons for their recommendations to you.

Even after you have signed, you have a 14-day cooling off period to allow you to change your mind.

Useful reading

Leaflets PM4 *You and Personal Pensions?* and PM5 *Pensions for the Self-Employed*, obtainable by ringing Pensions Info-Line on T:0845 731 3233.

Stakeholder Pensions and Decision Trees; Personal Pensions Mis-selling: The Facts and *FSA Guide to Pensions*, obtainable by calling the FSA on T:0845 606 1234.

Leaflet IR 78 *Personal Pensions*, from any tax office.

Types of investment policy

There are four different types of investment policy: with-profits, unit-linked, deposit administration and non-profit policies.

With-profits policies. These are one of the safest types of pension investments. They guarantee you a known minimum cash fund and/or pension on your retirement and, while the guaranteed amount is not usually very high, bonuses are added at various intervals.

Unit-linked policies. These are less safe but offer the attraction of potentially higher investment returns.

Deposit administration policies. These lie somewhere between with-profits and unit-linked policies in terms of their risk/reward ratio. They operate rather like bank deposit accounts, where the interest rate is credited at various intervals.

Non-profit policies. Although they provide a guaranteed pension payment, the return on investment is usually very low. Normally only recommended for people starting a plan within five years of their retirement.

Choosing the right policy. Great care is needed when choosing the organisation to invest your pension savings. Once you have committed yourself, you will not usually be able to change without considerable financial penalty. Before deciding, you should compare several companies' investment track records. Although no guarantee of their future performance, you might usefully look for evidence of good, consistent results over a period of 10 to 20 years.

Another point to scrutinise are the charges, including commission, you will have to pay. Normally, the best arrangement to keep the cost down is to pay a series of single premiums at one go or as a 'single recurring premium' contract.

Rather than try to work everything out yourself, you might do better to consult an Independent Financial Adviser (IFA).

Stakeholder Pensions

Stakeholder pensions were launched on 6 April 2001. While essentially targeted at those earning between £10,000 and £20,000, they are available to anyone except individuals in a final salary scheme whose earnings are over £30,000.

They are very similar to personal pensions but with the advantage that they are required to meet specified government standards, including limiting maximum annual charges (excluding financial advice) to 1 per cent.

Whereas until very recently pension contributions were always linked to earnings, a major change is that anyone with a stakeholder scheme can invest up to £3,600 a year, regardless of how much or how little they earn – or even if they have no earnings at all. A husband or wife could make contributions for a non-earning partner. Those wishing to contribute more than £3,600 are able to do so but the same age/percentage-of-earnings rules will apply as those governing personal pensions (see page 36).

All contributions paid will be net of basic rate tax with the pension provider reclaiming the tax from the Inland Revenue. Higher rate taxpayers will need to reclaim the excess tax through the self-assessment system. N.B. Because of the tax relief, the actual cost of a contribution worth £3,600 is £2,808 (£2,160 for higher rate taxpayers).

Among other welcome features, savers are able to stop, start or alter payments without penalty. Those contributing over £3,600 who become unemployed or stop work and who, therefore, might have lost out because of the age/earnings link applicable to higher contributions, will be allowed to continue paying in the same amounts as before for up to five years.

Although not many people are expected to do so, you could contribute to both a stakeholder pension and to a personal, or other, money purchase pension, provided the total of your annual contributions does not exceed £3,600; or, in the case of higher contributions, is within the limit allowed under the personal pension rules. Equally, those (typically early retirees) who are already drawing an occupational pension can, if they wish, start contributing to a stakeholder pension.

As with personal pensions, stakeholder pensions will be able to be taken at any age between 50 and 75.

How to obtain. Stakeholder pensions are widely available from banks, post offices, insurance companies and other financial institutions. Although the basic charges may not be very different between one provider and another, you are nevertheless strongly advised to investigate at least two or three plans and ask for much the same sort of information as you would if you were considering a personal pension.

This is even more important if you are actually thinking of switching from a PP to a stakeholder pension or, as is possible, to have a stakeholder as well as a PP.

Advantages and drawbacks. As general wisdom, many experts are of the view that if you are happy with your present arrangements, you might be best staying as you are. Though stakeholders are likely to be cheaper, you could face penalties if you terminate your existing scheme early. Equally, if you are thinking of switching from an employer's money purchase scheme, you will lose the extra contributions that your employer is making on your behalf.

Against this, the flexibility you would get with a stakeholder to alter or stop payments without penalty is attractive, as is the fact that regardless of your former earnings you can continue paying into a stakeholder for an extra five years after you stop work.

Since weighing up the pros and cons of making a change is not easy, you are strongly recommended to get expert advice.

For general information (but not financial advice) you can ring the OPAS stakeholder helpline on T:0845 601 2923.

A lump sum?

Members of company pension schemes and people with individual pension policies can take a tax-free lump sum when they retire. The maximum normally permitted is one-and-a-half times average final salary.

Taking a lump sum reduces your pension but if you invest the money wisely, you could end up with a higher income. Alternatively, as many people do, you could use the capital for a worthwhile project such as improving your home.

Deciding whether a lump sum makes economic sense depends mainly on: your age, tax status, life expectancy – and whether you can manage on a smaller annual pension. It is not 'an all or nothing' decision. You can choose between: not taking a lump sum, taking the maximum allowed or taking just a portion (whatever sum you decide). An accountant or other financial adviser would help you work out the sums.

Pension rights if you continue to work after retirement age

When you reach normal retirement age, you will usually stop making contributions into your company pension scheme, even if you continue working. You will then probably have three choices:

■ You can continue working, draw your company pension and put some of your earnings into a separate scheme. People over 60 can invest up to 40 per cent of their earnings tax free into a pension plan.

Provided you joined your current scheme before 13 March 1989 (or an existing scheme where you were employed before 1 June 1989) you also have the following choices:

■ You can leave your pension in the fund where it will continue to earn interest until you retire. In most private schemes, you can expect to receive an extra 9 per cent for every year that you delay retirement.
■ You can leave your pension in the fund, as described above, and also contribute to a personal pension provided your contributions do not exceed the Inland Revenue limit.

Pensions for women

Women who have worked all their adult lives and paid full Class 1 contributions should get a full basic pension in their own right at the age of 60. The current amount is £72.50 a week.

Women who have only worked for part of their adult lives may not have enough contributions to get a full basic pension on their own record. Instead, they may receive a reduced pension or one based on their husband's contributions; or one topping up the other. A wife entitled to a reduced pension on her own contributions can claim it at 60, regardless of whether or not her husband is receiving his pension.

Married women who have never worked are entitled to a pension on their husband's contributions. In money terms, the value is about 60 per cent of their husband's basic pension. There are several important conditions, however.

Firstly, women can only get a pension based on their husband's contributions if he is in receipt of a basic pension. He must have reached 65 and have retired. Also, the wife herself must be over 60.

If she is still under 60 when her husband claims his state pension and does not work or her earnings do not exceed £53.05, he should be able to obtain a supplement of around £43.40 to his pension, on the grounds of having a wife to support. If the couple are living apart, the earnings limit for the wife is £43.40. Your Social Security office will be able to advise.

In contrast, if a wife has had her sixtieth birthday but her husband has not yet reached 65 (or has decided to defer his retirement), she must wait until her husband retires to receive her share of the married couple's pension.

Reduced rate contribution

Many women retiring today have paid a reduced rate of NI contribution, also known as 'the small stamp'. This option was withdrawn in 1978 but women who had already chosen to pay the reduced rate were allowed to continue. If you have only ever paid reduced rate contributions, you are not entitled to a basic pension in your own right but must rely on your husband's contributions for the married couple's pension.

Home responsibilities protection (HRP)

Men and women who have been unable to work regularly because they have had to stay at home to care for children and/or a disabled or elderly person may be able to safeguard their pension by claiming Home Responsibilities Protection. The person you are caring for must come into one of the following categories:

- A child under 16 for whom you are getting child benefit
- Someone whom you are looking after regularly for at least 35 hours a week, who is in receipt of attendance allowance, constant attendance allowance or disability living allowance

- Someone – for example, an elderly person – for whom you have been caring at home and in consequence have been getting income support
- A combination of the above situations.

HRP can only be given for complete tax years (6 April to 5 April), so if you simply gave up work for a few weeks in order to help out, you would be unlikely to qualify. Additionally, HRP cannot be used to reduce your total working life to below 20 years. To claim, ask your Social Security office for form CF 411.

Graduated pension. At best, this would only be a small amount. See page 20 for more detail.

Additional pension (SERPS). This too is described earlier in the chapter. See page 19.

Divorced wives

If you have a full basic pension in your own right, this will not be affected by divorce. However if despite having worked for a good number of years, you have insufficient contributions to qualify for a full pension, you should contact your Social Security office, quoting your pension and national insurance numbers. You may possibly be able to obtain the full single person's pension, based on your ex-husband's contributions.

Your right to use your ex-husband's contributions to improve or provide you with a pension depends on your age and/or whether you remarry before 60. As a general rule, you can use your ex-husband's contributions for the years you were married (i.e. until the date of the decree absolute). After that, unless you remarry, you are expected to pay your own contributions until you are 60.

If you are over 60 when you divorce, whether you remarry or not, you can rely on your ex-husband's contributions. If you remarry before 60, you cease absolutely being dependent on your former husband and instead, your pension will be based on your new husband's contribution record.

A divorced man can rely on his former wife's contribution record during the years they were married to improve his basic pension.

For further information, ask your local Inland Revenue office for leaflet CA 10, *National Insurance for Divorced Women*.

Decisions regarding **occupational pensions** (including SERPS) are determined by the Courts. A judge could direct a pension scheme to make maintenance payments and/or allocate part of a lump sum to a divorced wife on the retirement or death of her ex-husband; or alternatively he could require the couple to share their occupational pension rights at the time of divorce. However, the fact that these options are available to the Courts does not necessarily mean that a judge would consider them appropriate in all cases.

Separated wives

Even if you have not lived together for several years, from a national insurance point of view you are still considered to be married. The normal pension rules apply including the fact that, if you have to depend on your husband's contributions, you will not be able to get a pension until he is both 65 and in receipt of his own pension.

If you are not entitled to a State pension in your own right, you will receive the dependant's rate of benefit. Once you are 60, you can draw the wife's pension of £43.40 a week, without reference to your husband.

If you are under 60 but your husband has reached 65 and is retired, he may be able to claim a dependency addition of £43.40 for you. He will not be able to do so if you are earning more than £43.40 a week.

If your husband dies, you may be entitled to one or more of the widowed persons' benefits described below.

Widows

There are three important benefits to which widows may be entitled: bereavement benefit, bereavement allowance and widowed parent's allowance. All are largely modelled on the former widows' benefits (widow's payment, widow's pension, widowed mother's allowance), with the important difference that all are now also applicable to widowed men. To claim the benefits, fill in Form BB 1, obtainable from any Social Security office. N.B. Widows who were already in receipt of the widow's pension before it was replaced by bereavement allowance in April 2001 are not affected by the change and will continue to receive their pension as normal.

Bereavement benefit. This is a tax-free lump sum of £2,000, paid as soon as a woman (man) is widowed provided that: (1) her husband had paid sufficient NI contributions (2) she is under state retirement age; or (3) if she is over 60, her husband had not been entitled to retirement pension. Her claim will not be affected if she is already receiving a State pension, provided this is based on her own contributions.

Bereavement allowance. This has replaced widow's pension and is for those aged between 45 and State pension age who do not receive widowed parent's allowance. As before, there are various levels of payment: full rate and age-related. The allowance is payable for 52 weeks. Receipt in all cases is dependent on sufficient NI contributions having been paid.

Full-rate bereavement allowance is paid to widows (also widowers) between the ages of 55 and 59 inclusive. The weekly amount is £72.50, which is the same as the current pension for a single person.

Age-related bereavement allowance is for younger widows/widowers, who do not qualify for the full rate. It is payable to widowed persons, who are aged between 45 and 54 inclusive when their partner dies. Rates depend on age and vary from £21.75 for 45 year olds to £67.43 for those aged 54.

Bereavement allowance is normally paid automatically once you have sent off your completed form BB 1, so if for any reason you do not receive it you should enquire at your local Social Security office.

As applies to widow's pension, widows who remarry, or live with a man as his wife, cease to receive bereavement allowance.

For further information, see leaflet *The New Bereavement Benefits*. See also chapter 12, page 185.

Widowed parent's allowance. This is paid to widowed parents with at least one child for whom they receive child benefit. The current value (2001/02) is £72.50 a week.

Retirement pension. Once a widow reaches 60, she would normally receive a State pension based on her own and/or her late husband's contributions.

If at the time of death the couple were already receiving the State retirement pension, the widow will continue to receive her share. An important point to remember is that a widow may be able to use her late husband's NI contributions to boost the amount she receives.

Other important points. Widows over 60 whose only income is their State pension, or less, may be entitled to claim Minimum Income Guarantee (see page 22, earlier in the chapter).

Separate from the basic pension, a widow may also receive money from her late husband's occupational pension, whether contracted in or out of SERPS. She may also get half of any of his graduated pension.

4

You May Pay Less Tax in Retirement

Unfortunately, much as we should like to leave this out, the taxman never seems to retire!

Unless you are on a very low income, you will almost certainly be paying income tax and possibly one or two other varieties of tax as well. Although for most retired people the issues are not particularly complex, a little basic knowledge can be invaluable.

Firstly, it will help you to calculate how much money (after deduction of tax) you will have available to spend. Understanding the broad principles could also help you save money, by not paying more in taxation than you need.

If you are lucky enough to be fairly wealthy or if some of the recent Budget changes give you cause to wonder whether you are managing your money as tax-efficiently as you might, you should talk to an accountant.

Income tax

This is calculated on all (or nearly all) your income, after deduction of your personal allowance; and in the case of older married people, of the married couple's allowance. The reason for saying 'nearly all' is that some income you may receive is tax free: types of income on which you do not have to pay tax are listed a little further on.

Most income, however, counts and you will be assessed for income tax on: your pension, interest you receive from most types of savings, dividends from investments, any earnings (even if these are only from casual work) plus rent from any lodgers, if the amount you receive exceeds £4,250 a year. Many social security benefits are also taxable.

The tax year runs from 6 April to 5 April the following year, so the amount of tax you pay in any one year is calculated on the income you receive (or are deemed to have received) between these two dates.

There are three different rates of income tax: the 10 per cent rate which applies to the first £1,880 of your taxable income; the 22 per cent basic rate tax which applies to the next slice of taxable income between £1,881 and £29,400; and the 40 per cent higher rate tax which is levied on all taxable income over £29,400.

All income tax payers will pay the 10 per cent rate on their first £1,880 of taxable income. Or put another way, for every £100 of your income that counts for income tax purposes up to £1,880, you have to pay £10 to the Exchequer – and are allowed to keep the remaining £90. If you are a basic rate taxpayer, the amount you have to pay the Exchequer increases (after the first £1,880) to £22; and if you are a higher rate taxpayer, it goes up to £40 for every £100 of your taxable income over £29,400.

In most Budgets, some of the figures change. Those quoted above – and elsewhere in the chapter – apply to the 2001/02 tax year.

Tax allowances

Personal allowance

Income tax is not levied on every last penny of your money. There is a certain amount you are allowed to keep before income tax becomes applicable. This is known as your personal allowance. Therefore, when calculating how much tax you will have to pay in any one year, you should first deduct from your total income the amount represented by your personal allowance (plus any additional or other tax allowance to which you may be entitled, see sections following). If your income is no higher than your personal allowance (or total of these allowances), you will not have to pay any income tax.

Everyone receives the same basic personal allowance, regardless of whether they are male, female, married or single; and regardless of whether any income they have comes from earnings, an investment, their pension or other source.

■   The basic personal allowance (2001/02) is £4,535.

People aged 65 and over may be entitled to a higher personal allowance, by virtue of their age. Those aged 75 and above may receive even more generous treatment.

The full amount is only given to people whose income does not exceed £17,600. People with higher incomes may still receive some age-related allowance but this is gradually withdrawn by £1 for every £2 of income above the income limit. People with income above a certain level do not receive any age allowance. This ceiling is known as the upper limit. But however large your income, your personal allowance can never be reduced below the basic personal allowance.

For those aged 65 to 74:

■ personal allowance is increased to £5,990.
■ the upper limit is £20,510.

For those aged 75 and older:

■ personal allowance is increased to £6,260.
■ the upper limit is £21,050.

N.B. Extra allowance linked to age is normally given automatically. If you are not receiving it but believe you should be doing so, you should write to your local tax office (see under Inland Revenue in the telephone directory) stating your age and, if married, that of your partner. If you have been missing out, you may be able to claim back anything you have lost for up to six years and should receive a tax rebate. The amounts have been altered several times since 1995/96, so any rebate would only apply to allowances that would have been due to you at the time.

Married couple's allowance

Married couple's allowance was abolished, except for older couples, at the start of the April 2000/01 tax year.

Those still entitled to receive the allowance are (1) couples where at least one of the partners was born before 6 April 1935 and (2) older newly-weds, provided that one of the partners is aged 65 or more at the time of the marriage and that their date of birth was before 6 April 1935. In both cases, to be eligible, a couple must live together, i.e. as opposed to being separated.

Similar to age-related personal allowance, couples on low income receive extra – and a higher amount still when either partner reaches 75.

A further point to note is that unlike the old basic married couple's allowance which could be shared equally between the spouses or trans-ferred in whole to the wife, the age/income-related addition always goes to the husband.

■ The current (2001/02) minimum married couple's allowance is £2,070
■ The higher income-related allowance for couples where both partners are under 75 and whose income is under £17,600 is £5,365.

- When either the husband or wife reaches 75, the allowance is increased to £5,435. The income limit, as before, is £17,600.

N.B. Three important points you should know:

- Married couple's allowance is restricted to 10 per cent tax relief.
- The increases based on age/income are normally given automatically. If couples are not receiving any extra but believe they should be, the husband should write to their local tax office stating their ages. If there has been a mistake, he will be given a rebate.
- A widowed partner, where the couple at time of death were entitled to married couple's allowance, can also claim any unused portion of the (married couple's) allowance in the year they became widowed.

Registered blind people can claim an allowance of £1,450 a year. If both husband and wife are registered as blind, they can each claim the allowance.

If you think you would be eligible, you should write to your local tax office with full relevant details of your situation. If you were entitled to receive the allowance earlier but for some reason missed out, you may be able to obtain a tax rebate.

Useful reading

For more detailed information about tax allowances, see the following Inland Revenue leaflets obtainable free from any tax office (see under Inland Revenue in the telephone directory).

- IR 90 *Tax Allowances and Reliefs*
- IR 121 *Income Tax and Pensioners*

Tax relief

Separate from any personal allowances, you can obtain tax relief on the following:

- A covenant for the benefit of a charity; or donation under the Gift Aid Scheme
- Contributions to occupational pensions, self-employed pension plans and other personal pensions
- Some maintenance payments, if you are divorced or separated and were aged 65 or older at 5 April 2000.

Mortgage interest relief. As most home-owners will know, mortgage interest relief was withdrawn on 6 April 2000.

The only purpose for which relief is still available is in respect of loans secured on an older person's home to purchase a life annuity. However to qualify, the loan must have been taken out (or at least processed and confirmed in writing) by 9 March 1999.

Borrowers in this situation can continue to benefit from the relief for the duration of their loan.

As before, the relief remains at 10 per cent on the first £30,000 of loan.

Self-employed and other personal pension plans. The rules are not the same for all types of pension plan. In particular, there are important differences between personal pensions (PPs) and retirement annuity contracts.

With a PP, you can pay the following amounts into your pension scheme and obtain tax relief:

- if you are aged 35 or under, 17.5 per cent of your earnings (up to a ceiling of £95,400)
- between the ages of 36 and 45, 20 per cent of your earnings
- between the ages of 46 and 50, 25 per cent
- between the ages of 51 and 55, 30 per cent
- between the ages of 56 and 60, 35 per cent
- ages 61 and over, 40 per cent

N.B. Since April 2001, you can make contributions up to £3,600 a year to a personal pension (PP) regardless of your age or earnings. If you wish to contribute more, you can do so under the rules described just above.

If you choose to take out a **stakeholder pension**, as with PPs, you can make contributions of up to £3,600 each tax year irrespective of your earnings (and even if you earn nothing at all). Contributions above £3,600 are subject to the same age and earnings-related limits as personal pensions, with the added advantage that contributions can continue for 5 years after earnings have ceased. You pay the contributions net of basic rate tax and your pension provider will then reclaim the tax from the Inland Revenue. Higher rate taxpayers will need to reclaim the additional tax via the self-assessment system.

Personal pension schemes started before 1 July 1988 are known as **retirement annuity contracts**. You can pay the following amounts into a retirement annuity and obtain tax relief (unlike PPs, there is no ceiling on earnings):

- if you are aged 50 or under, 17.5 per cent of your earnings
- between the ages of 51 and 55, 20 per cent

- between the ages of 56 and 60, 22.5 per cent
- ages 61 and over, 27.5 per cent.

Ages are calculated at the beginning of the tax year.

Maintenance payments. Tax relief for maintenance payments was withdrawn on 6 April 2000.

Individuals receiving maintenance payments are not affected and will continue to receive their money free of income tax. Those who had to pay tax under the pre-March 1988 rules now also receive their payments free of tax.

Most individuals paying maintenance, however, will face higher tax bills. This applies especially to those who set up arrangements before the March 1988 budget. While previously they got tax relief at their highest rate, since 6 April 2000 they no longer get any relief at all. An exception has been made in cases where one, or both, of the divorced/separated spouses was aged 65 or over at 5 April 2000. Those paying maintenance are still able to claim tax relief – but only at the 1999/2000 standard rate of 10 per cent.

Tax credits

There are three tax credits that could be of possible interest: the Working Families Tax Credit (WFTC), the Disabled Person's Tax Credit (DPTC) and the new Children's Tax Credit (CTC) which came into being in April 2001.

Both the **Working Families Tax Credit** and the **Disabled Person's Tax Credit** are payments given to individuals who, despite working at least 16 hours a week, only have a modest income and limited savings.

An essential condition to receive the Working Families Tax Credit is that the family, or lone parent, must have at least one child in full time education, aged under 19, living with them.

The Disabled Person's Tax Credit is only given to individuals on low income with an illness or disability to help them return to work.

Most recipients get the money in their pay packet. However the self-employed receive the payment direct from the Inland Revenue, as can a non-earning partner (i.e. if a couple so chooses) in the case of WFTC.

Application forms can be obtained from post offices, job centres, Benefits Agency offices, Citizens' Advice Bureaux and Inland Revenue Tax Enquiry Centres. Or for further information, telephone the following helplines: Working Families Tax Credit helpline T:0845 609 5000; Textphone: 0845 606 6668. Disabled Person's Tax Credit helpline T:0845 605 5858. Textphone: 0845 608 8844.

The **Children's Tax Credit** is not a payment as such but a tax relief, which reduces the amount of tax payable by a family, or lone parent, with at least one child under 16 who lives with them for all or part of the year.

The credit is worth up to £520 a year but is clawed back progressively for higher-rate taxpayers who lose the relief completely if their annual income reaches £41,735. The rule applies if either one of the parents is a higher-rate taxpayer.

To obtain the Children's Tax Credit application form, ring T:0845 300 1036. Or for further information, see booklet CTCR/1 *Children's Tax Credit*, obtainable from any tax office.

Come April 2003, a new **Pensioner Credit** is being introduced designed to give those with modest savings extra relief against tax. It is expected to benefit single people with incomes of up to £135 a week and couples with incomes up to £200.

Tax-free income

Some income you may receive is entirely free of tax. It is not taxed at source. You do not have to deduct it from your income, as in the case of personal allowances. Nor do you have to go through the formality of claiming relief on it.

If you receive any of the following, you can forget about the tax angle altogether – at least as regards these particular items:

- Disability living allowance
- Industrial injuries disablement pension
- Income support (in some circumstances, e.g. when the recipient is also getting jobseeker's allowance, income support would be taxable)
- Housing benefit
- Council tax benefit
- Any extra which may be added to your state pension if you support children under 16
- All pensions paid to war widows (plus any additions for children)
- Pensions paid to victims of Nazism
- Certain disablement pensions from the armed forces, police, fire brigade and merchant navy
- Annuities paid to the holders of certain gallantry awards
- £10 Christmas bonus (paid to pensioners)

- National Savings Premium Bond prizes
- SAYE bonuses
- Winnings on the football pools and on other forms of betting
- Rental income of up to £4,250 a year from letting out rooms in your home.
- Winter fuel payment (paid to pensioners)
- Income received from certain insurance policies, including mortgage payment protection and permanent health insurance
- All income received from savings in an ISA (Individual Savings Account).

Other tax-free money

The following are not income, in the sense that they are more likely to be 'one off' rather than regular payments. However, as with the above list they are tax free:

- Virtually all gifts (in certain circumstances you could have to pay tax if the gift is above £3,000 or if, as may occasionally be the case, the money from the donor has not been previously taxed).
- Redundancy payment, or a golden handshake in lieu of notice, up to the value of £30,000.
- Lump sum commuted from a pension with a maximum figure of £143,100.
- A matured endowment policy.
- Accumulated interest from a Tax Exempt Special Savings Account (TESSA) held for 5 years.
- Dividends on investments held in a Personal Equity Plan (PEP).
- Compensation money paid to people who were mis-sold personal pensions.
- Compensation paid to those who were mis-sold free standing AVCs (FSAVCs). To qualify for exemption from tax, the money must be paid as a lump sum as opposed to in annual payments.

Income tax on savings

Until recently, all income from savings was taxed at a normal rate of 20 per cent and at 40 per cent for higher rate taxpayers.

Perversely, the 10 per cent starting rate of tax was not applicable to savings income such as bank and building society interest but instead only applied to earned and pension income. In consequence many less well off people, including in particular thousands of pensioners, were paying more tax than they would otherwise have been due.

Happily in the March 2000 budget, the Chancellor extended the 10p starting rate of income tax to include savings income. This means that any income – whether from earnings, a pension or savings – now qualifies towards the 10p starting rate of tax. For 2001/02, this is on the first £1,880 of taxable income.

If you largely rely on your savings income and so believe you are among those who have paid excess tax, you can reclaim this from the Inland Revenue. For advice on what to do, call the Taxback helpline on T:0845 077 6543. You might also find it helpful to see 'Reclaiming tax overpaid', page 55.

Income tax on other investments

For most investments on which you are likely to receive dividends, tax will already have been deducted before the money is paid to you.

If you are a basic rate taxpayer, the money you receive will be yours in its entirety and you will not have to worry about making deductions for tax.

If you pay tax at the higher rate, you will have to pay some additional tax and should allow for this in your budgeting.

Exceptionally, there are one or two types of investment where the money is paid to you gross – without the basic rate tax deducted. These include National Savings income bonds, capital bonds, the NS Investment Account and, since 6 April 1998, all gilt interest (people who prefer to receive gilt interest net can request to do so). As with higher rate taxpayers, you will need to save sufficient money to pay the tax on the due date.

Avoiding paying excess tax on savings income

Banks and building societies automatically deduct the normal 20 per cent rate of tax from interest before it is paid to savers. As a result most working people, except higher rate taxpayers, can keep all their savings without having to worry about paying additional tax.

While convenient for the majority, a problem is that some 4 million people on low incomes – including in particular many women and pensioners – are unwittingly paying more tax than they need.

Those most affected are non-taxpayers (anyone whose taxable income is less than their allowances) who, although not liable for tax, are having it taken from their income before they receive the money.

Non-taxpayers can stop this happening quite simply by requesting their bank and/or building society to pay any interest owing to them gross, without deduction of tax at source.

If applicable, all you need do is to request form R85 from the institution in question or Inland Revenue Enquiry Centre, which you will then need to complete. If you have more than one bank or building society account, you will need a separate form for each account. Forms are also included in booklet IR 110 *A Guide for People with Savings*, obtainable from any tax office or from your bank/building society; or by telephoning the IR helpline on T:0845 077 6543.

People who have filled in an R85 should automatically receive their interest gross. If your form was not completed in time for this to happen, you can reclaim the tax from your tax office after the end of the tax year in April.

Reclaiming tax overpaid

If you are a non-taxpayer and have not yet completed an R85 form (or forms), you are very likely to be eligible to claim a tax rebate.

However, as stated earlier, this may also apply if you only pay tax at the 10 per cent starting rate; or if, since becoming retired, most of your income now comes from either taxed investments or bank/building society interest.

If any of these circumstances apply and you believe that the probability is that you could be due a refund, best advice is to ring the special **Taxback Helpline** on T:0845 077 6543 who will send you a copy of *A Guide for People with Savings*, together with a claim form and, if relevant, copies of form R85 for you to complete and give to your bank/building society.

Mistakes by the Inland Revenue

The Inland Revenue sometimes also makes mistakes. Normally, if they have charged you insufficient tax and later discover the error, they will send you a supplementary demand requesting the balance owing. However, under a provision known as the 'Official Error Concession', if the mistake was due to a fault by the Inland Revenue, it is possible that you may be excused the arrears. However, you would need to convince the IR that you could reasonably have believed your tax affairs were in order. Also, the IR would need to have been tardy in notifying you of the arrears (i.e. more than 12 months after the end of the tax year in which the IR received the information indicating that more tax was due).

As part of the Citizen's Charter, the Inland Revenue has appointed an independent Adjudicator to examine taxpayers' complaints about their dealings with the Revenue.

Complaints appropriate to the Adjudicator are mainly limited to the way the Inland Revenue has handled someone's tax affairs, for example: excessive delay, errors, discourtesy or how discretion has been exercised. In deciding fair treatment, the Adjudicator has power to recommend the waiving of a payment or even the award of compensation if, as a result of error by the Inland Revenue, the complainant had incurred professional fees or other expenses.

Before approaching the Adjudicator, taxpayers will be expected to have tried resolving the matter with their local tax office or, if this fails, with the Regional Office.

For further information, see IR booklet, Code of Practice 1, *Mistakes by the Inland Revenue*, available from tax offices.

Or contact the Adjudicator's office for information about referring a complaint. The address is: **The Adjudicator's Office**, 3rd Floor, Haymarket House, 28 Haymarket, London SW1Y 4SP. T:020 7930 2292.

Tax rebates

When you retire, you may be due for a tax rebate. If you are, this would normally be paid automatically, especially if you are getting a pension from your last employer. The matter could conceivably be overlooked: either if (instead of from your last employer), you are due to get a pension from an earlier employer; or if you will only be receiving a State pension – and not a company pension in addition.

In either case, you should ask your employer for a P45 Form. Then, either send it – care of your earlier employer – to the pension fund trustees; or, if you are only getting a State pension, send it to the tax office together with details of your age and the date you retired. Ask your employer for the address of the tax office to which you should write.

Post-war credits

Post-war credits are extra tax that people had to pay in addition to their income tax between April 1941 and April 1946. The extra tax was treated as a credit to be repaid after the war. People who paid credits were given certificates showing the amount actually paid.

In cases where the original credit holder has died without claiming repayment and the Post War Credit certificate is still available, repayment can be made to the next of kin or personal representative of the estate.

Interest is payable on all claims at a composite rate of 38 per cent. The interest is exempt from income tax.

All claims should be sent to the **Special Post War Credit Claim Centre** at: Inland Revenue, HM Inspector of Taxes – PWC Centre V, TY Glas, Llanishen, Cardiff CF4 5TX.

Capital gains tax (CGT)

You may have to pay capital gains tax if you make a profit (or to use the proper term, gain) on the sale of a capital asset, for example: stocks and shares, jewellery, any property that is not your main home and other items of value.

CGT only applies to the actual gain you make, so if you buy shares to the value of £25,000 and sell them later for £35,000 the taxman will only be interested in the £10,000 profit you have made.

Not all your gains are taxable. There is an exemption limit of £7,500 a year: so if during the year your total gains amount to £9,000, tax would only be levied on £1,500.

Additionally, certain items are free altogether of capital gains tax; and others, such as the sale of a family business, get special treatment. Details are given a little further on.

A very important point for married couples to know is that as a result of independent taxation each partner enjoys his/her own annual exemption of £7,500. This means in effect that, provided both partners are taking advantage of their full exemption limit, a couple can make gains of £15,000 a year free of capital gains tax. However, it is not possible to use the losses of one spouse to cover the gains of the other.

Transfers between husband and wife are tax free, although any income arising from such a gift will of course be taxed. Income would normally be treated as the recipient's for tax purposes.

Gains are variously taxed at: the 10p starting rate, the 20 per cent basic rate, or at 40 per cent for higher rate taxpayers; or a mixture of rates, i.e. in instances where a gain, or gains, pushes part of an individual's income into a higher rate bracket.

Longer-held assets, however, are taxed more lightly. In place of indexation, which was withdrawn in the March 1998 Budget, there is now a taper which reduces the rate of capital gains tax, year by year, on assets held for 3 years or longer. The rate for higher rate taxpayers reduces from 40 per cent to 24 per cent on assets held for 10 years or more (i.e. after 6 April 1988). The rate for basic rate taxpayers reduces from 20 per cent to 13.8 per cent. Assets acquired before 17 March 1998 get a bonus year on the taper, so qualifying them for the maximum reduction after 9 years, instead of 10.

Business assets, which include among one or two other categories all shares held in unquoted companies and shares held by employees in quoted trading companies, are taxed more lightly still – reducing to a bottom rate of 10 per cent after 4 years. The 4-year taper applies to shares held from 6 April 1998 provided these were not sold before the rules came into effect on 6 April 2000.

N.B. The Chancellor recently announced that, as from April 2002, the holding period for maximum taper relief is being reduced from 4 to 2 years.

Free of capital gains tax

The following assets are not subject to capital gains tax and do not count towards the £7,500 gains you are allowed to make:

- Your main home (but, see note below)
- Your car
- Personal belongings up to the value of £6,000 each
- Proceeds of a life assurance policy (in most circumstances)
- Profits on UK Government stocks
- National Savings Certificates
- SAYE contracts
- Building society mortgage cash backs
- Futures and options in gilts and qualifying corporate bonds
- Personal Equity Plan (PEP) scheme
- Gains from assets held in Individual Savings Account (ISA)
- Premium Bond winnings
- Football pool and other bettings winnings
- Gifts to registered charities
- Small part disposals of land (limited to 5 per cent of the total holding, with a maximum value of £20,000).
- Gains on the first disposal of Enterprise Investment Scheme shares.

Your home. Your main home is usually exempt from capital gains tax. However, there are certain 'ifs and buts' which could be important.

If you convert part of your home into an office or into self-contained accommodation on which you charge rent, that part of your home which is deemed to be a 'business' may be separately assessed – and CGT may be payable when you come to sell it. (CGT would not apply, if you simply take in a lodger who is treated as family, in the sense of sharing your kitchen or bathroom).

If you leave your home and let it for profit – perhaps because you have decided to live permanently with a friend – under tax law, the property would be treated as an investment and, subject to certain exemptions, would be assessed for CGT when it was sold.

Part of the argument hinges on owner occupation. If you are not living in the property (or a part of it which you have let out for rent), then the house – or that section of it – is no longer considered to be your main home. People who are liable for CGT in these circumstances can apply for special relief of up to £40,000. If you leave your home to someone else who later decides to sell it, he/she may be liable for CGT when the property is sold (although only on the gain since the date of death). There may also be inheritance tax implications, so if you are thinking of leaving or giving your home to someone, you are strongly advised to consult a solicitor or accountant.

If you own two homes, only one of them is exempt from CGT, namely the one you designate as your 'main residence'.

Selling a family business. If you sell all or part of your business when you retire, you may not have to pay tax on the first £100,000 of capital gain with a further exemption allowed of one-half of gains between £100,001 and £400,000. To get maximum relief, you must be aged at least 50 and must have completed the sale before 6 April 2002, as retirement relief is being gradually reduced year by year until April 2003, when it will be finally withdrawn. If you sell the business between 6 April 2002 and 5 April 2003, you will still get some retirement relief but the above tax exemptions will then be halved. If you are forced to retire early through ill health, the age rules may be applied less strictly and you may still be entitled to retirement relief.

There are also other possible tax benefits if you re-invest the profits within three years in another unquoted company.

Since this is a very complex field, before either retiring or selling shares, you are strongly recommended to seek professional advice.

Selling shares should not be confused with giving part of your family business to the next generation, which has been made easier under the inheritance tax rules. However, the advice about seeking professional help still applies.

Useful reading

For further information about capital gains tax, see leaflet CGT 1 *Capital Gains Tax: an Introduction*, available from any tax office:

Self-assessment

If you are one of the nine million people who needs to complete a tax return, you will probably be all too familiar with self-assessment. It mainly affects the self-employed and higher rate taxpayers but could apply if part of your remuneration is not fully taxed under PAYE or if you have other income that is not fully taxed at source.

Even if you have never needed to complete a tax return before, it is possible that when you retire this will become necessary. This is most likely if you become self-employed or if you receive income that has not already been fully taxed – in which case, it is your responsibility to inform your local tax office who, depending on the amount of money involved, will advise you whether you will need to fill in a tax return.

Whatever the situation, all taxpayers now have a legal obligation to keep records of all their different sources of income and capital gains. These include:

- details of any earnings, bonuses, expenses and benefits in kind you received
- bank and building society interest
- dividend vouchers and/or other documentation showing gains from investments
- pension payments, i.e. both State and occupational/private pension
- misc. income, such as freelance earnings, maintenance payments, taxable social security benefits
- payments against which you claim tax relief (e.g. charitable donations, contributions to a personal pension).

If you are self-employed or a partner in a business, as well as the above list, you also need to keep records of all your business earnings and expenses, together with sales invoices and receipts.

Self-assessment is optional. If you think the calculations are too complicated or that you might be at risk of making a mistake, you can leave it to the Revenue to work out the amount of tax you are due. There are penalties for late submissions, so it is important not to miss the critical dates. For further information, see IR booklets SA/BK3 *Self-Assessment – A Guide to Keeping Records for the Self-employed*; SA/BK4 *Self-Assessment – A General Guide to Keeping Records* and SA/BK8 *Self-Assessment – Your Guide*, obtainable from any tax office or by calling the Self-Assessment Leafletline on T:0845 900 0444.

N.B. It is possible that although in the past you received a self-assessment form, you did not receive a new one last April. This may be because the rules were recently changed to take individuals with incomes of just over £500 that had not been taxed at source out of the system. You may be one of the lucky ones but, if you did not receive a form and are in any doubt, it would be advisable to check with your local tax office to avoid the risk of a penalty for late payment.

Inheritance tax

Inheritance tax applies to money and/or gifts passed on at time of death (or sometimes before).

The first £242,000 of an individual's estate is tax free. Amounts over this are taxed at a single rate of 40 per cent. However, before any tax is calculated, there are a number of exemptions and other concessions of which perhaps the most important is that there is no tax on gifts or inheritance between spouses. Also, most family-owned businesses are exempted from inheritance tax; as are most life-time gifts, providing certain important conditions are met.

Gifts or money up to the value of £3,000 can be given annually free of tax, regardless of the particular date they were given.

Additionally, it is possible to make small gifts to any number of individuals free of tax, provided the amount to each does not exceed £250.

For exemption on other life-time gifts to apply, the gift must have been made at least seven years before the donor's death and moreover, it must have been unconditionally given; or to use the jargon, 'without reservation'. A gift in which the donor retains an interest or some direct control – for example, a house 'given' to his children in which the parent continues to live – does not qualify for exemption.

The seven-year period is not totally inflexible, in that there is taper relief: in other words, a tapering rate of tax, according to how close to the seven year limit the death of the donor occurred. Gifts made within three years of death do not qualify for any relief and the tax will have to be paid in full.

For gifts made more than three years before death, the rates are as follows:

- Death between 3 and 4 years of gift, IHT reduced by 20%
- Death between 4 and 5 years of gift, IHT reduced by 40%
- Death between 5 and 6 years of gift, IHT reduced by 60%
- Death between 6 and 7 years of gift, IHT reduced by 80%

Quite apart from IHT, capital gains tax may have to be paid on any asset you left to a beneficiary, or as part of your estate, which is subsequently sold. The Inland Revenue treats such assets as having been acquired at the date of death and at their prevailing market value at the time. By the same token, CGT will have to be paid on any gain that has built up on an asset you gave away during your lifetime and which is subsequently sold. Not surprisingly perhaps, tax specialists say that there are legitimate ways of minimising the liability.

Another very important consideration is the need to make a will. Neglect to do so can have serious consequences for those whom you might wish to benefit. For further information, see 'Making a will', (page xxx).

If you have already written a will, you are strongly recommended to have this checked by a professional adviser to ensure that you do not give money unnecessarily to the taxman.

For further information about inheritance tax, see booklets *An Introduction to Inheritance Tax* (IHT 3), *Inheritance Tax on Lifetime Gifts* (IHT 2) and *Alterations to an Inheritance Following a Death* (IHT 8), obtainable from any tax office.

Expenditure taxes

Other than the duty on alcohol, tobacco and petrol, there are three main expenditure taxes: VAT, insurance premium tax, and air passenger duty.

VAT. You pay this automatically on most goods and services, at a flat rate of 17.5 per cent. N.B. Exceptionally, VAT on both domestic fuel and the installation of energy-saving materials is only 5 per cent. The 5 per cent rate also applies to children's car seats and to central heating systems, grant-funded by government, to help less well off pensioners and other needy households.

Insurance Premium Tax (IPT). Tax is 5 per cent and applies to premiums paid on all general insurance, **except** travel insurance and insurance bought as part of a package, e.g. when included with a warranty. In both these cases, the IPT is 17.5 per cent.

Air passenger duty. Except for flights from airports in the Scottish Highlands and Islands, where the duty has been abolished, passengers are charged £5 on economy fares, and £10 duty on business and first-class fares, on flights within the UK and to other destinations within the European Economic Area (EEA). The duty on economy air fares to all other destinations is £20; £40 on business and first-class fares.

UK pensions paid abroad

- Technically your State pension could be subject to income tax, as it derives from the UK. In practice, if this is your only source of UK income, tax would be unlikely to be charged.
- If you have an occupational pension, UK tax will normally be charged on the total of the two amounts.
- If the country where you are living has a double tax agreement with the UK, your income may be taxed there – and not in Britain. Britain now has a double tax agreement with most countries. For further information, check the position with your local tax office.
- If your pension is taxed in the UK, you will be able to claim part of your personal allowance as an offset. A married man living with his wife may also be able to claim part of the married couple's allowance, if by virtue of their age they would still be eligible to receive it (see 'Married couple's allowance', page xx).
- Both State and occupational pensions may be paid to any country. If you are planning to retire to Australia, Canada, New Zealand or South Africa, you would be advised to check on the up-to-date position regarding any annual increases you would expect to receive to your pension. Some people have found the level of their pension 'frozen' at the date they left Britain, while others have been liable for an unexpected tax overseas.
- Any queries about your pension should be addressed to the International Payments Office, Pensions and Overseas Benefits Directorate, Tyneview Park, Newcastle upon Tyne NE98 1BA. T:0191 218 7777.

5

Investment Wisdom

Investment is a subject for everyone. One of your most important aims must be to make your existing money work for you so you will be more comfortable in the years ahead.

Many articles on retirement planning concentrate almost exclusively on ways of boosting your immediate income to compensate for your loss of earnings. Frankly, this is very short-sighted. An equally if not even more critical concern must be to safeguard your long term security, even if this means some minor sacrifice to your current standard of living.

The likelihood is that you will live for 20 years or longer after you retire and your partner may live longer still. Your financial planning must therefore be aimed not just for your sixties but also for your eighties and maybe even your nineties.

Inflation is another essential factor that must be taken into account since, unless you plan carefully, this could badly affect your standard of living after a few years.

Sources of investable funds

You do not need to be in the director league to have money for investment. Possible sources of quite significant capital include:

- Commuted lump sum from your pension
- Insurance policies, designed to mature around your retirement
- Profits on your home, if you sell it and move to smaller, less expensive accommodation
- Redundancy money, golden handshake or other farewell gift from your employer
- Sale of SAYE and other share option schemes.

General investment strategy

Investments differ in their aims, tax treatment and the amount of risk involved. Ideally you should plan to acquire a mix of investments, designed variously: to provide some income to supplement your pension and also some capital appreciation to maintain your standard of living long term.

Except for annuities and National Savings, which have sections to themselves, the different types of investment are listed by groups, as follows:

- Variable interest accounts
- Fixed interest securities
- Equities
- Long-term lock-ups.

As a general strategy, it is a good idea to aim to choose at least one type of investment from each group.

Annuities

Definition. A normal life annuity is a very simple investment to understand. You pay a capital sum to an insurance company and in return are guaranteed an income for life. The money is paid to you at fixed intervals and will remain exactly the same year in, year out. Payments are calculated according to life expectancy tables and for this reason an annuity is not really a suitable investment for anyone under 70. Other than your age, the key factor affecting payments is the level of interest rates at the time you buy: the higher these are, the more you will receive.

An annuity would probably give you more immediate income than any other form of investment. But whether you actually get good value depends on how long you live. When you die, your capital will be gone. So if you die a short while after signing the contract, it will represent very bad value indeed. On the other hand, if you live a very long time, you may more than recoup your original capital.

As a precaution against early death, it is possible to take out a capital protected annuity, an annuity which includes a guaranteed payment period or an annuity which transfers to your partner for the duration of his/her life. Any of these options will reduce the annuity income you receive but could be worth considering if your primary concern is to give your partner (or other beneficiaries) added security.

The difference between the three choices is briefly as follows. **Capital protected annuities** pay out any balance left from your original investment after deduction of the annuity payments paid to date. **Annuities with a guarantee period** are normal life annuities with the important difference that if you die before the end of the guaranteed period, the payments for the remaining years (of the guaranteed period) will go to your partner or other beneficiary. **Annuities incorporating a spouse's benefit** pay out the annuity income to you during your lifetime and will then pass to your partner for the remainder of his/her life.

There are also other types of annuity, such as capital and income plans which pay you a small income, say, for a 10-year period, at the end of which your capital is returned.

Annuities, such as those described above, which you choose to buy as a purely optional purchase should not be confused with **pension-linked annuities** which are a required purchase for people with personal pensions or with other types of money purchase plans. For further information about compulsory purchase annuities, see page 27.

Tax. Income tax on optional annuities is relatively low, as part of the income is allowed as a return on capital which is not taxable. Pension-linked annuities are fully taxable.

How to obtain. You can buy an annuity either direct from an insurance company or via an intermediary, such as an independent financial adviser (IFA). But shop around, as the payments vary considerably. For names of IFAs, contact: **IFA Promotion Ltd.**, T:0117 971 1177; **The Money Management National Register of Fee-based Advisers**, T:020 7074 1200.

Assessment. Safe. Attractive if you live to a ripe old age. But highly vulnerable to inflation. Sacrifice of capital that might otherwise benefit successors.

National Savings

It is very easy to invest in National Savings, as all you need do is go to the post office for information or telephone the National Savings Sales Information Unit on T:0845 964 5000 (Monday – Friday, 8 a.m. to 8 p.m.; Saturday, 9 a.m. to 1 p.m.); all calls are charged at local rates.

Most types of investment offered by NS are broadly similar to those provided by banks and other financial institutions. So rather than explain in detail the exact terms and conditions of, say, a National Savings Investment Account, it is easier to suggest that you pick up the relevant leaflet at the post office counter or telephone the above number.

The main investments offered by National Savings are:

- **Ordinary account**. Pays a fairly low rate of variable interest. You can invest between £10 and £10,000. The first £70 of interest each year is free of tax. Ask for booklet DNS 760.
- **Investment account**. You can invest between £20 and £100,000. Interest is taxable but paid in full without deduction of tax at source. Ask for booklet DNS 761.
- **Income bonds**. Pay a fairly attractive rate of interest, increasing with larger investments. Interest which is taxable is paid gross. You can invest between £500 and £1 million. Ask for booklet DNS 767.
- **National Savings Certificates**. Offer a fixed rate of interest that is tax free. You can invest from £100 to £10,000. For maximum benefit, you must hold the certificates for five years. Ask for booklet NSA 762.
- **Index-linked Certificates**. You can invest from £100 to £10,000. You get interest (at time of writing 1.65 per cent) plus the increase in the Retail Prices Index. To get best return, certificates must be kept for five years. Interest is tax free. Ask for booklet NSA 763.
- **2-year Tax Free Certificates**. Both fixed interest and index-linked National Savings certificates are now available for 2-year terms. As with the 5-year certificates, you can invest from £100 to £10,000. You can hold the 2-year versions in addition to any 5-year certificates you have.
- **Capital Bonds**. These offer a guaranteed interest rate, providing you do not withdraw your money before five years. The one big drawback is that tax on the interest has to be paid annually – with higher bills every year as the interest grows – until you actually receive any money. Minimum purchase is £100. Ask for booklet NSA 768.
- **Children's Bonus Bond**. Bonds are sold in multiples of £25 and the maximum purchase per child in the current issue is £1,000. Both interest and bonus, which will be paid after five years, are free of income tax. Interested parents and grandparents should ask for booklet NSA 769.
- **Fixed Rate Savings Bonds**. These are lump sum investments that earn guaranteed rates of interest over set periods of time, from 6 months to 2 years. You can decide whether to have your interest paid out or reinvested into your bond, either on a monthly or annual basis, or at the end of the term. You can also choose where the interest is paid. The minimum investment is £500; the maximum, £1 million.

- **5-year Pensioners Guaranteed Income Bond**. A special bond for savers aged over 60, offering a guaranteed rate of interest for five years. The income which is taxable is paid monthly. Minimum purchase is £500; the maximum, £1 million. Ask for booklet NSA 773.
- **1 year and 2-year Pensioners Guaranteed Income Bond**. Similar to the above 5-year pensioners bond, with the important difference that to obtain full value the money is only locked up for one or two years respectively.

National Savings also offers a cash mini ISA with a government approved CATmark.

Variable interest accounts

Few people who rely on interest from their savings to provide them with extra income in their retirement will need reminding that interest rates can go down as well as up! This is not a reason for forgetting all about variable interest accounts (when interest rates were high, they provided one of the best homes for many people's money); but it is essential to understand how such accounts work – together with their advantages and drawbacks.

Recent changes. Most banks and building societies have introduced interest bearing current accounts. Although an improvement on the standard current account, these are not suitable for keeping large savings for more than a short time. If you are tempted to switch to an interest bearing account, check what charges apply if you dip into over-draft. You should also enquire whether you are being offered 'tiered rates' – those paying the top rate of interest applicable on all your funds; or the less attractive 'banded rates' – those with two levels of interest, with a lower amount paid on, say, the first £500 or £1,000 and the higher rate only on funds above that amount.

A further point to investigate is whether there is a fixed monthly or other charge. This can sometimes change at fairly short notice. You should check your monthly statement carefully and consider moving your account if you are dissatisfied.

While it is perhaps stating the obvious, you should also keep an eye on what rate of interest you are being paid – and compare it to the rates being offered by other savings institutions. This has become very much easier as all advertisements for savings products must now quote the Annual Equivalent Rate (AER). Unlike the former variety of different ways of expressing interest rates, the AER provides a true comparison taking into account the frequency of interest payments and whether or not interest is compounded.

Finally, you should also know about ISAs (see a couple of pages over).

Definition. Other than the interest bearing accounts described above, these are all savings or deposit accounts (share accounts in building societies) of one form or another, arranged with banks, building societies and the National Savings Bank. They include among others: basic deposit accounts, high interest accounts and fixed term deposit accounts.

Your money collects interest while it is on deposit, which may be credited to your account or for which you may receive a regular cheque. Some institutions pay interest annually; others pay monthly. If you have a preference, this is a point to check. The rate of interest will vary, up or down, according to the level of national interest rates. While you may get a poor return on your money if interest rates drop, your savings will nearly always be safe as you are not taking any kind of investment risk.

Access. This depends on the type of account you choose: you may have a cheque book and withdraw your money when you want; you may have to give about a week's notice; or if you enter into a term account, you will have to leave your money deposited for the specified period. In general, accounts where a longer period of notice is required earn a better rate of interest.

Sum deposited. It is not usually sensible to consider a deposit account unless you have a minimum of £100. For certain types of account, the minimum investment could be anything from £500 to about £5,000.

Tax. With the exception of both TESSAs and cash ISAs (see pages 69 and 75), which are tax-free, and of the National Savings Bank, where interest is paid gross, tax is deducted at source – so you can spend the money without worrying about tax. However, you must enter the interest on your tax return; and if you are a higher rate taxpayer, you will have additional liability.

Non-taxpayers can arrange to have their interest paid in full by completing a certificate which enables the financial institution to pay the interest gross.

N.B. Until recently, people who would normally only have paid tax at the 10p starting rate were at a major disadvantage as the 10 per cent rate only applied to earned and pensions income – and not to savings income such as bank and building society interest. As a result, although not basic rate taxpayers, many less well off people were still being charged the full 20 per cent rate on their savings income. Happily this injustice has now been put right and the 10 per cent rate now equally applies to savings income. If you largely rely on your savings income and believe you are or have been paying excess tax, you can reclaim this from the Inland Revenue. For further information see 'Income tax on savings', page 53 and 'Reclaiming tax overpaid', page 55.

Choosing a deposit account

There are two key choices: the type of deposit account you want and where to invest your money. The basic points to consider are as follows:

Basic deposit account. This attracts a relatively low rate of interest. But it is both easy to set up and very flexible, as you can add savings when you like and can usually withdraw your money without any notice. It is a much better option than simply leaving your money in a current account and is a good temporary home for your cash if you are saving short-term for, say, a holiday. However, it is not recommended as a long-term savings plan.

High interest deposit account. Your money earns a higher rate of interest than it would on an ordinary deposit account. You will need to deposit a minimum sum, which could be around £500 to £1,000. While you can always add to this amount, if your basic deposit drops below the required minimum, your money will stop earning the higher interest rate.

Fixed term deposit account. You deposit your money for an agreed period of time, variously from a few months to over a year. In return, you will normally be paid a superior rate of interest.

There is a minimum investment of roughly £1,500 to £10,000. If you need to withdraw your money before the end of the agreed term, there are usually hefty penalties. Before entering into a term account, you need to be sure that you can afford to leave the money on deposit.

You will also need to take a view about interest rates: if they are generally low, your money may be better invested elsewhere.

It is important to keep a note of the date when the agreement expires. As a rule, your money will no longer earn preferential rates after the term has ended. The bank or other institution may not notify you in advance and may, quite legitimately, simply credit you with the normal interest rates after the contract's expiry.

Tax Exempt Special Savings Account (TESSA). TESSAs were withdrawn at the start of the tax year on 6 April 1999. Although it is no longer possible to open a TESSA account, anyone with an existing TESSA at the time of their withdrawal can continue to pay into it under the old rules for its full five-year life without this counting against their annual subscription limit to an ISA. The capital from a maturing TESSA can then be transferred into an ISA.

N.B. If you are continuing to make payments into your TESSA, you might be advised to check what interest rates you are being paid. Some savers have found that these have been disproportionately slashed and that, even taking into account the fact that the interest would be tax-free on the maturity of their TESSA, their money would be better invested elsewhere.

Fixed interest securities

In contrast to variable interest accounts, fixed interest securities offer a fixed rate of interest which you are paid, whatever happens to interest rates generally. Since most are only suitable for those who can afford riskier investments, we only describe gilts as these are guaranteed by the government.

Gilt-edged securities

Definition. These are stocks which guarantee both the interest payable and the repayment price promised on a given date.

The maturity date can be anything from a few months to 20 years or longer. Stocks are variously known as: short-dated, medium-dated and long-dated. A further category is undated. Additionally, there are index-linked gilts.

Prices are quoted per £100 of nominal stock. For example, a stock may be quoted as: 10 per cent Treasury Stock 2004, 99 1/2 – 100 1/4. In plain English, this means the following:

- 10 per cent represents the interest you will be paid. You will receive the interest payment twice yearly, 5 per cent each time.
- You are buying Treasury Stock.
- The maturity date is 2004.
- To buy the stock, you will have to pay £100.25p (i.e.100 1/4).
- If you want to sell, the market price you will get is £99.50p (i.e. 99 1/2).

Gilts are complicated by the fact that you can either retain them until their maturity date, in which case the government will return the nominal value in full. Or you can sell them on the Stock Exchange at market value.

Prices are affected by current interest rates. If interest rates are at 6 per cent, a gilt with a guaranteed interest payment of 10 per cent is a very attractive buy – so the price will rise. Conversely, if interest rates are 10 per cent, a guaranteed interest payment of 6 per cent is a poor proposition, so the price will drop.

Index-linked Gilts are designed to shield investors against inflation: they pay very low interest but are redeemable at a higher price than the initial purchase price, as their value is geared to the cost of living. They are most valuable when inflation is high.

Tax. Before April 1998 income tax was normally deducted at source, except in the case of gilts bought on the National Savings Stock Register (NSSR) where the interest was paid gross. Today however, gilt interest from whatever source is paid gross. This does not mean that you avoid paying it, simply that you must allow for a future tax bill before spending the money. Recipients who prefer to receive the money net of tax can request for this to be arranged.

A particular attraction of gilts is that they are free of capital gains tax.

How to buy. You can buy gilts through banks, building societies, a stockbroker or financial intermediary. Or you can get a form at the post office and purchase gilts through the Bank of England, which has recently taken over the postal gilts buying and selling service from the National Savings Stock Register. In all cases, you will be charged commission.

A booklet *Investing in Gilts*, together with purchase forms, is obtainable from: The Chief Registrar, **Bank of England**, Southgate House, Southgate Street, Gloucester GL1 1UW. Freephone: 0800 818614.

Assessment. Gilts normally pay reasonably good interest and offer excellent security, in that they are backed by the government. You can sell at very short notice and the stock is normally accepted by banks as security for loans, if you want to run an overdraft.

However, gilts are not a game for amateurs as, if you buy or sell at the wrong time, you could lose money; and if you hold your stock to redemption, inflation could take its toll on your investment.

Gilt plans. This is a technique for linking the purchase of gilt-edged securities and with-profit life insurance policies to provide security of capital and income over a 10 to 20-year period. These plans are normally obtainable from financial intermediaries.

Equities

These are all stocks and shares, involving varying degrees of risk. They are designed to achieve capital appreciation as well as give you some regular income. They are easy to purchase thanks to the increase in the number of Internet and telephone share-dealing facilities. Most allow you to get your money out within a week.

Equities can be excellent money-spinners but there is always some risk. They include: ordinary shares, unit trusts and ISAs.

Ordinary shares listed on the Stock Exchange

Definition. Public companies issue shares as a way of raising money. When you buy shares and become a shareholder, you participate in the profits through a dividend. In bad years, it is possible that no dividends will be paid. In good years, dividends can increase substantially.

The money you invest is unsecured. This means that, quite apart from any dividends, your capital could be slashed in value – or if the company goes bankrupt, you could lose the lot. Against this, if the company performs well you could greatly increase your wealth.

You can buy shares via a stockbroker, a share shop, the securities department of your bank or via an Internet or telephone share-dealing service. In all cases, you will be charged commission and stamp duty. You will be issued with a share certificate which you or your adviser must keep, as you will have to produce it when you wish to sell.

You may be advised to use a nominee account, as being cheaper and more convenient. The one big disadvantage is that you may miss out on access to various benefits – including shareholders' perks.

Tax. The standard rate of tax on income from share dividends is 20 per cent, with higher rate taxpayers required to pay 40 per cent. Quite apart from income tax, if during the year you make a profit of over £7,500 from selling shares, you would be liable for capital gains tax.

Changes in the taxation of share dividends

Until recently, companies paid advanced corporation tax (ACT) and investors enjoyed the benefit of a 20 per cent tax credit on their dividends from shares. However, all that has now changed. ACT was abolished on 6 April 1999, as were tax credits – with the exception of those applying to dividends held in PEPs and ISAs. These tax credits have now been halved in value to 10 per cent and are due to be abolished altogether in April 2004.

Although most people investing in shares will not have to pay any more tax, their dividend income will be reduced. Non-taxpayers, including many pensioners, have been especially badly hit as they can no longer reclaim any tax credit direct.

Unit trusts and OEICs

Definition. Unit trusts and OEICs (open-ended investment companies, a modern equivalent of unit trusts) offer an alternative to buying shares on the Stock Exchange. Your money is pooled in a fund, run by managers, who invest the proceeds in a wide range of shares and other securities. The advantages are that: it is usually less risky; it is very simple to understand; you get professional management and there are no day-to-day decisions to make. Also, every fund is required by law to have a trustee (called a depository in the case of OEICs) to protect investors' interests.

The minimum investment in some of the more popular funds is £500; in others, it can be as high as £10,000. Some funds allow you to purchase units, or shares, for smaller amounts on a regular monthly plan.

There is often a front end fee of around 5 per cent but this varies however, from group to group and from fund to fund.

Investors' contributions to the fund are divided into units (shares in OEICs) in proportion to the amount invested. As with ordinary shares, you can sell some or all of your investment by letting the fund manager know that you wish to do so.

How to obtain. Units and shares are purchased from: banks, building societies, insurance companies, stockbrokers or specialist investment fund providers, with whom you can either deal directly or via an independent financial adviser.

For a list of unit trusts, OEICS and other information contact the **Unit Trust Information Service**, 65 Kingsway, London WC2B 6TD. T:020 8207 1361.

Tax. Units and shares invested through an ISA have special advantages. Otherwise tax treatment is identical to ordinary shares.

Assessment. An ideal method for smaller investors to buy stocks and shares: both less risky and easier.

Investment Trusts are companies that invest in the shares of other companies, providing a spread of risk. You can buy investment trusts through a saving and investment scheme which is simple and cheap.

Split capital trusts separate capital growth and income growth. These can be mixed and matched to meet your needs during retirement.

For a free information pack, write to **The Association of Investment Trust Companies,** Durrant House, 8–13 Chiswell Street, London EC1Y 4YY.

Personal equity plan

PEPs have ceased to be available since 6 April 1999, when they were withdrawn by the government to be replaced by the Individual Savings Account (ISA). However, although it is no longer possible to acquire a PEP, anyone with an existing PEP (or number of PEPs) before their withdrawal can retain it under the old rules and continue to enjoy the same tax advantages as before. Individuals can, if they wish, also subscribe to an ISA – see below.

For those who may have forgotten the detail, PEPs allow you to buy shares in a range of investments including corporate bonds and investment trusts, with the advantage that all income and gains are exempt from tax. The money has to be invested through an authorised manager, for example: a bank, building society or financial intermediary.

Since April 2001, PEPs have been made more flexible as a result of the government aligning the rules with those of ISAs. The main changes are: (1) there is no longer a distinction between general and single company PEPs, so investors who wish do so can merge the two (2) investors are now able to invest in the listed shares of companies anywhere in the world and (3) investors can now transfer part of a PEP to another PEP manager and not just the whole PEP as before.

Tax. PEPS are free of both income tax and capital gains tax.

Assessment. The tax advantages are attractive, although the halving of dividend tax credits has removed some of the shine. Also no shares are without risk and even corporate bond PEPs are not totally risk-free as capital values could fall. While probably remaining worthwhile, especially for higher rate taxpayers, the charges could be a critical factor in deciding whether a PEP is still the best place for your money.

Individual Savings Account (ISA)

Definition. ISAs are the new savings accounts which the government launched on 6 April 1999 as a replacement for PEPs and TESSAs. They contain many of the same advantages in that all income and gains generated in the account are tax free.

As with PEPs and TESSAs, there is a subscription limit – with the maximum annual amount you can put into an ISA being £7,000. From April 2006, the maximum amount will be reduced to £5,000.

An ISA can contain any, or all, of the following:

- up to £3,000 in cash;
- up to £1,000 in life assurance;
- stocks and shares.

The £3,000 cash element can include National Savings, bank and building society accounts and also supermarket savings accounts.

There are two types of ISA: a maxi ISA and a mini ISA. It is important to understand the difference because, once you have made a choice, you cannot change your mind. The essential point is that with a maxi ISA you can invest more, or all, of your money in shares, whereas with a mini ISA you are limited to a maximum of £3,000.

You are not obliged (as is required with TESSAs) to keep savings/investments in the account for a fixed period but instead can make withdrawals at any time. However, once you have subscribed the maximum in a year, you will not be allowed to put in any more, regardless of how much is withdrawn.

All money held in an ISA – whether cash, life assurance or stocks and shares – must be administered by an authorised manager, or managers. If you choose to have a maxi ISA, the whole of your ISA must be with a single manager. In the case of a mini ISA, you could subscribe to separate mini ISAs for cash savings, life assurance and stocks and shares with different managers.

As a further safeguard, the government has introduced a voluntary benchmark guaranteeing that the ISA being offered meets approved standards with regard to cost, access, terms and conditions. The sign to look for is called a CATmark.

Tax. ISAs are completely free of all income tax and capital gains tax. However, you should be aware that a 20 per cent charge is levied on all interest accruing from non-invested money held in an ISA that is not specifically a cash ISA.

Assessment. ISAs offer a simple, flexible way of starting, or improving, a savings plan. The tax advantages are attractive, although will become rather less so when tax credits are finally abolished in 2004. Although the CATmark should be helpful as a guarantee of standards, investment in stocks and shares (which is not essential but over the years has proved the best way of making savings grow) always carries some element of risk.

Useful reading

The FSA Guide to Individual Savings Accounts, available free from the FSA, T:0845 606 1234.

Long-term lock-ups

Certain types of investment, mostly offered by insurance companies, provide fairly high guaranteed growth in exchange for your under-taking to leave a lump sum with them or to pay regular premiums for a fixed period, probably 10 years. Many are linked with some form of life assurance cover.

Life assurance policies

Definition. Life assurance can provide your successors with money when you die; or it can be used as a savings plan to provide you with a lump sum on a fixed date.

There are three basic types of life assurance: whole life policies, term policies and endowment policies.

Whole life policies are designed to pay out on death. In its most straightforward form, the scheme works as follows: you pay a premium every year and, when you die, your beneficiaries receive the money.

As with an ordinary household policy, the insurance only holds good if you continue the payments. If one year you did not pay and were to die, the policy could be void and your successors would receive nothing.

Term policies involve a definite commitment, i.e.: you elect to make regular payments for an agreed period, say ten years. If you die during this period, your family will be paid the agreed sum in full.

It is possible to arrange for the benefit to be paid out as regular income. This is known as **family income benefit**. The payments will cease at the end of the insured term. If you die after the end of the term, your family will normally receive nothing.

Many people argue that such policies, while eminently sensible when children are growing up, are one expense that can cheerfully be dropped on retirement. This could be short-sighted. A big problem for many widows is that, when their husband dies, part of his pension dies with him. A lump sum or regular income plan could make all the difference in helping to bridge the gap. Alternatively – and for some this could be a more attractive option – whole life or term can be converted into an endowment policy.

Endowment policies are essentially a savings plan. You contract to pay regular premiums over 10 or 25 years and receive a lump sum at the end.

Once you have committed yourself, you have to go on paying every year, as there are heavy penalties if you stop. This is especially true during the early years. The terms should be clearly spelt out on the sales literature.

An important feature of endowment policies is that if you die before the policy matures, the remaining payments are excused and your successors will be paid a lump sum on your death.

Endowment policies have long been popular as a way of making extra financial provision for retirement. The amount of money you stand to receive can vary hugely, however, depending on the charges. Aim to compare at least three policies before choosing.

Options. Both whole life policies and endowment policies offer two basic options: with profits or without profits. Very briefly the difference is as follows:

Without profits. This is sometimes known as 'guaranteed sum assured'. It means that the insurance company guarantees you a specific fixed sum which you know in advance and is what you – or your successors – will be paid.

With profits. You are paid a guaranteed fixed sum plus an addition, based on the profits that the insurance company has made by investing your payments. The basic premiums are higher and the profits element is not known in advance. If the insurance company has invested your money wisely, a 'with profits' policy provides a useful hedge against inflation. If its investment policy is mediocre, you could have paid higher premiums for very little extra return.

Unit linked. This is a refinement of the 'with profits' policy, in that the investment element of the policy is linked in with a unit trust.

Other basics. Premiums can normally be paid monthly or annually. Size of premium varies, depending on: the type of policy you choose and the amount of cover you want. As very general guidance, £35–£50 a month would probably be a normal starting figure. Higher premiums often give better value as relatively less of your contribution is swallowed up in administrative costs.

Most policies require you to sign a declaration of health. It is very important that this should be honestly completed: if you make a claim and it is discovered that you gave misleading information, the insurance company could refuse to pay.

How to obtain. Policies are available through banks, insurance companies, independent financial advisers (IFAs) and building societies. The biggest problem for most people is the enormous choice. Another difficulty can be understanding the small print: terms which sound very similar may obscure important differences which could affect your benefit.

It is usually advisable to consult an IFA, who should give you full details of the risks, benefits, charges and his/her reasons for recommending a particular policy. For help in finding an IFA in your area, contact: **IFA Promotion Ltd**., 17–19 Emery Road, Brislington, Bristol BS4 5PF. T:0117 971 1177. See also 'Where to go for Financial Advice', page 88.

The **Association of British Insurers (ABI)** has a number of useful information sheets on life assurance. Contact ABI, 51 Gresham Street, London EC2V 7HQ.

Tax. The proceeds of a qualifying policy – whether taken as a lump sum or in regular income payments (as in the case of family income benefit) – are free of all tax.

Assessment. Life assurance is normally a sensible investment, whether the aim is to provide death cover or the benefits of a lump sum to boost your retirement income. It is very attractive from a tax angle. Also, certain policies provide good capital appreciation (although recent bonuses have tended to be disappointing). However, you are locked into a long term commitment. So, choosing the right policy is very important. Shop around, take advice and, above all, do not sign anything unless you are absolutely certain that you understand every word.

Alternatives to surrendering a policy

As already mentioned, there are heavy penalties if you surrender an endowment policy before its maturity. Some people, either because they can no longer afford the payments or for some other reason, wish to terminate the agreement – regardless of any losses they may make/or investment gains they sacrifice.

Instead of simply surrendering the policy, people in this situation have two alternative options, both of which stand to yield them a higher return than surrender. The one is to sell the policy by auction; the other to sell it outright.

Auctioneers typically charge a registration fee (about £50) plus commission on the excess (they make at auction) above the surrender value quoted. The risk is minimal, since if the policy fails to reach its reserve it can still be surrendered in the normal way.

Market makers who buy policies offer a cash price that at very least would be higher than the surrender value. To be of interest to them, the policy would need to meet their purchasing criteria, e.g. age of policy and length of time to maturity.

A full list of appropriate financial institutions and dealers that buy and sell mid-term policies is obtainable from the **Association of Policy Market Makers**. T:020 7739 3949.

Investor protection

Anyone selling investment products, or policies, must by law be authorised by a regulatory body, all of which have strict rules. For your protection, there are a number of essentials you should know.

- Never deal with any adviser without knowing by whom they are authorised. The most likely body is the FSA, although at time of writing it could still be the PIA, SFA or IMRO (see section below).
- Businesses may either promote their own in-house investment plans (unit trusts, insurance policies and so on) or they must act as independent consultants and have no vested interest in any product they recommend. Make sure you know which your adviser is.
- To give 'best advice', independent consultants need to understand your requirements in detail. Before asking you to sign, they should give you a 'reason why' letter explaining why they believe their recommendation best meets your needs.
- Some advisers charge fees for their time. Some are paid in commission. Others receive a salary with commission on top. You are at perfect liberty to ask which applies and to enquire what the commission level is.
- All charges including management fees should be clearly stated on the literature. Make sure before signing that you understand the total amount you will have to pay.

A new single regulatory authority

Finding out whether investment businesses are authorised or not and checking up on what information they are required to disclose should start to become very much easier. As from 1st December 2001, all the existing self-regulating organisations (including the PIA, IMRO and

SFA) are due to be merged under the Financial Services Authority with the purpose of improving investor protection and of providing a single contact point for enquiries. The address, should you need to contact the FSA, is: **Financial Services Authority**, 25 The North Colonnade, Canary Wharf, London E14 5HS. T:0845 606 1234 (calls charged at local rate).

A Single Ombudsman Scheme

As from 1st December 2001, there will also be a single Financial Ombudsman Service (FOS), which will replace the various schemes which currently deal with complaints about financial services. The schemes concerned are: Banking Ombudsman, Building Societies Ombudsman, Insurance Ombudsman, Personal Insurance Arbitration Service, PIA Ombudsman, Investment Ombudsman, SFA Complaints Bureau (and Arbitration Schemes) and FSA Complaints Unit.

A big advantage of there being a single ombudsman scheme is that the FOS will cover complaints across almost the entire range of financial services and products – from banking services, endowment mortgages and personal pensions to household insurance and stocks and shares. The list will equally include unit trusts and OEICs, life assurance and FSAVCs.

Complaints

If you have a complaint against an authorised firm, in the first instance you should take it up with the firm concerned: you may be able to resolve the matter at this level, since all authorised firms are obliged to have a proper complaints-handling procedure.

If this gets nowhere or if after eight weeks you are still dissatisfied, you can approach whichever is the most relevant ombudsman or complaints scheme listed above or alternatively (and this would probably be simpler), contact the new Financial Ombudsman Service which to all intents and purposes is already operating.

Either way, an Ombudsman will investigate the matter on your behalf and if he finds your complaint is justified may require the firm to pay compensation which, depending on your losses, could be up to £100,000.

If you disagree with the Ombudsman's decision, this does not affect your right to go to court should you wish to do so.

For further information, contact the **Financial Ombudsman Service (FOS)**, South Quay Plaza, 183 Marsh Wall, London E14 9SR. T:0845 080 1800.

6

Where to go for Financial Advice

If there is one golden rule when it comes to money matters, it must be: when in doubt, ask. This applies as much if it is a term with which you are unfamiliar, as whether you are wondering how best to invest your savings.

When thinking about retirement planning, it is important to get as much advice as possible. Even if you have never done so before, there is no cause to feel hesitant about approaching financial advisers.

As someone who may shortly be retiring, you are seen as a very attractive potential client, especially if you are a member of a pension scheme with a sizeable commuted lump sum to invest.

Before making contact, it is generally a good idea to try to sort out your priorities, for example: whether you are looking for capital growth or whether your main objective is to increase your income. Also, if you have any special plans such as helping your grandchildren or spending money on home improvements, these too should be thought through in advance as they could affect the advice you receive.

Another reason for doing some advance thinking is that, whereas some advisers – for example, insurance brokers – do not specifically charge you for their time, others such as accountants and solicitors charge fees by the hour. Drinking coffee in their office and musing about the future delights of retirement may be a pleasant way of spending the afternoon but it can also work out to be pretty costly!

Choosing an adviser

When choosing an adviser, there are usually four main considerations: respectability, suitability, price and convenience.

Where your money is concerned, you cannot afford to take unnecessary risks. Merely establishing that an individual is a member of a recognised institution, while a basic safeguard, is insufficient recommendation if you want to be assured of dealing with someone who will personally suit you. The principle applies as much with friends, as with complete strangers.

If you are thinking of using an adviser whom you do not already know in a professional capacity, you should certainly check on their reputation and, ideally, talk to some of their clients. No one who is any good will object to your asking for references.

Also, quite apart from general competence, professional help is very much a question of 'horses for courses'. Just as you would hardly consult a divorce lawyer if you were buying a house, so too in the financial field most practitioners have different areas of expertise. It is, therefore, important to establish that your adviser has the particular capability you require.

It generally makes sense to choose a firm that is reasonably accessible. If you live in a part of the country, where the choice of financial advisers is limited, you can approach one of the organisations listed on the following pages that maintain a register of members – or, you could ask your bank manager to recommend someone suitable.

Finally, you should be aware that some specialist advisers earn commission, so have a vested interest in any sale they make. Also some brokers and dealers are tied agents for a specific company so can only promote their own in-house products. To know where you stand, you should ask any agent whom he represents; whether he is a tied agent; and why in particular he is recommending X product, or policy, as being most suitable for you.

Accountants

Accountants are specialists in matters to do with taxation. They can help you avoid paying more tax than you need and can assess the tax effects of different types of investment you may be considering. Likewise, they can help you with the preparation of tax returns and if you are thinking of becoming self-employed, they will be able to assist you with some of the practicalities – such as registering for VAT and establishing a system of business accounts.

If you need help in finding a suitable accountant, any of the following should be able to assist:

Institute of Chartered Accountants in England and Wales, PO Box 433, Chartered Accountants' Hall, Moorgate Place, London EC2P 2BJ.

Institute of Chartered Accountants of Scotland, CA House, 21 Haymarket Yards, Edinburgh EH12 5BH.

Institute of Chartered Accountants in Ireland, Chartered Accountants House, 87–89 Pembroke Road, Ballsbridge, Dublin 4.

Association of Chartered Certified Accountants, 29 Lincoln's Inn Fields, London WC2A 3EE.

Complaints. Anyone with a complaint against an accountant can write to the Secretary of the Institute's Investigating Committee who, if the complaint is valid, will refer the matter to the Disciplinary Committee.

Banks

Most people need no introduction to the clearing banks since, if they have a bank account, they are probably being regularly bombarded with literature. Yet despite this, many customers do not actually realise what a comprehensive service their bank provides.

In addition to the normal account facilities, all the major high street banks offer investment, insurance and tax planning services, as well as advice on drawing up a will.

Abbey National Plc, 215–229 Baker Street, London NW1 6XL. Offers a range of savings, mortgage, pension, current account, medical and other insurance products; and also loans for such items as home improvements, or to finance a holiday. There are various savings accounts paying tiered rates of interest, as well as a variety of savings bonds – including a retirement income bond for over 55s – plus also a range of ISAs.

Additionally, Willis National (at 10 Trinity Square, London EC3A 3AX. T:020 7488 8383) offers independent financial planning advice for those nearing retirement or already retired.

Full details of all Abbey National services can be obtained from any high street branch; or call T:0800 555100.

Barclays Bank Plc, 54 Lombard Street, London EC3P 3AH. Offers customers a range of accounts to suit a variety of personal savings requirements. Their financial planning services (available through subsidiary companies) include: personal investment advice, investment management, stockbroking, unit trusts, life assurance, pensions, personal taxation, wills and trusts.

You can either write to the above address or apply through your local branch.

HSBC Personal Financial Services, Poultry, London EC2P 2BX. Offers a comprehensive choice of financial products – including OEICs, ISAs and life assurance – which are selected according to a customer's requirements by a personal financial planning manager.

HSBC also offers an Estate Planning Service which includes preparation of a will, drawing up trusts and administering customers' estates.

Any HSBC branch can arrange a meeting if you would like to discuss these services.

Lloyds TSB Group, 71 Lombard Street, London EC3P 3BS. Lloyds TSB offers a wide range of financial services, including: current and savings accounts; health and home insurance; investment management; and also life assurance, through Scottish Widows. Details are available at all Lloyds TSB branches. If you would like to discuss your insurance requirements in any detail, you can also ring the following special numbers: (health) 01633 818200; (home insurance) freephone 0800 750750.

NatWest, 135 Bishopsgate, London EC2M 3UR. Can advise on a wide range of banking and financial planning services for retirement. To make an appointment, contact your local NatWest branch or call free on T:0800 255 200, between 8 a.m. and 8 p.m. weekdays, or 9 a.m. to 6 p.m. Saturdays.

Royal Bank of Scotland, 42 St Andrew Square, Edinburgh EH2 2YE. Offers a comprehensive range of current accounts and savings products. There is a personal tax service with work charged according to its complexity and also a free financial planning service provided by Royal Scottish Assurance, the Royal Bank of Scotland's life assurance, pensions and investment company. Further information can be obtained from any branch of the Bank.

Additionally, the Bank's Private Trust and Taxation Department gives free advice on making a will, although the usual legal fees apply if you proceed; write to The Royal Bank of Scotland, Freepost, PO Box 31, Edinburgh EH2 0BG.

New high street and other banking services. As the many lucky people who received windfalls will know, since 1997 several building societies have converted to banks, including: The Halifax, Woolwich, Alliance & Leicester, Bristol & West, Bradford & Bingley and Northern Rock. Full information about their services should be obtainable from your local branch.

Among other new trends, there has been an explosion of both telephone and Internet banking services, many of which at time of writing were offering very competitive interest rates.

Complaints

The Banking Ombudsman acts as an independent arbitrator, who aims to resolve complaints by individuals and small businesses about banking services from the 125 banks which come within the scheme. These include all the main high street banks. His decisions are binding on banks and he is empowered to award compensation of up to £100,000. The service is free.

Complaints can be handled on most aspects of personal banking, including bank credit cards, as well as maladministration or undue delays in dealing with wills and trusts. However, except where there has been maladministration, the Ombudsman's powers do not extend to commercial decisions on the grant of an overdraft or loan.

The address to which to write is: **The Banking Ombudsman**, South Quay Plaza, 183 Marsh Wall, London E14 9SR. T:0845 080 1800.

N.B. As explained earlier, from 1st December 2001, the Banking Ombudsman is due to become part of the new single ombudsman scheme called the Financial Ombudsman Service (FOS). The address is the same as that of the Banking Ombudsman. For further information, see Financial Ombudsman Service page 91.

Insurance sales people

The insurance business covers a very wide range from straightforward policies – such as motor or household insurance – to the rather more complex areas, including life assurance and pensions. Quite apart from the confusion of the enormous choice of policies and the importance of ensuring that you understand the conditions laid down in the small print, a further difficulty is the number of different categories of people – agents, salesmen, brokers, independent financial advisers (IFAs) – who may try to sell you insurance.

Insurance brokers

Unless you are already dealing with an insurance company that suits you, you would normally consult an insurance broker for advice about the more everyday type of insurance, e.g. motor, medical, household and holiday insurance.

A broker should be able to help you choose the most suitable policies, help you determine how much cover you require and explain any technical terms contained in the documents. He can also assist with any claims and advise you when renewals are necessary. An essential point to check before proceeding is that the firm the broker represents is registered with the General Insurance Standards Council.

Although a condition of registration is that a broker must deal with many insurers and therefore be in a position to offer a wide choice of policies, most companies pay insurance brokers on a commission basis; so, it is possible that you could be offered advice that is not totally unbiased.

Generally speaking, you are safer to use a larger brokerage with an established reputation. Also, before you take out a policy, it is advisable to consult several brokers in order to get a better feel for the market. **The British Insurance Brokers Association** (BIBA House, 14 Bevis Marks, London EC3A 7NT) can send you a list of brokers in your area.

Complaints. If you have a complaint against a registered insurance broker you could contact the General Insurance Standards Council. They will investigate the matter and, if they think your complaint is justified, will seek to get redress for you. You should write to: **General Insurance Standards Council**, 110 Cannon Street, London EC4N 6EU. T:020 7648 7800.

Another useful source is the Association of British Insurers, which represents 438 companies, who between them handle about 90 per cent of business done by British insurance companies. If you are in dispute with one of the Association's members, the ABI will ensure that your complaint is dealt with at top level. The address is: **Association of British Insurers (ABI)**, 51 Gresham Street, London EC2V 7HQ. T:020 7600 3333.

There is also an **Insurance Ombudsman**. He exists mainly to help private policy holders but can take up the cudgels on behalf of small businesses provided consent is given by the insurance company. The company in question must be a member of the Ombudsman Scheme. You can find this out from your insurance company, broker, a CAB or from the Ombudsman's Bureau direct. While there is no charge for the service, you must contact the Ombudsman within six months of the insurance company's final decision on the dispute.

The Ombudsman has power to make awards up to £100,000 and while he can adjudicate on most issues, some matters such as third party claims are outside his scope. He will also not be able to help if legal proceedings have been started.

For further information, contact: **The Insurance Ombudsman Bureau**, South Quay Plaza, 183 Marsh Wall, London E14 9SR. T:0845 080 1800. N.B. In common with the Banking Ombudsman and others, the Insurance Ombudsman is due to become part of the single Financial Ombudsman Service. The address is the same as that of the Insurance Ombudsman Bureau. For further information, see page 91.

Independent financial advisers (IFAs)

IFAs specialise in advising on products and policies with some investment content including, for example, endowment policies, life assurance and unit trusts. They help you work out what type of policy would be most suitable for you and where you could obtain best value for money. They can also handle all the arrangements for you.

Before committing yourself, you should ask your adviser a number of questions, including: by whom they are regulated; what charges are involved; what commission, if any, he/she will be getting; whether it is possible you could lose money; how soon surrender values will equal premiums paid; and why, in particular, you are being recommended to buy the policy or investment in question. Your adviser should provide you with both a 'key features document' and a 'reason why letter', answering all these points. It is essential to read them carefully and if there is anything you do not understand, you should certainly ask!

While commission is still the norm, an increasing number of financial advisers now offer a fee-based service, rather in the manner of an accountant or solicitor. This means, of course, that clients are charged an up-front fee. But against this, they are not forfeiting the often very much larger sum – deducted from their investment – that the IFA would have received. Because of the way some insurance companies operate, fee-charging advisers may still receive the commission in the first instance but will then – depending on the client's preference – either rebate it back to them in cash or (and this could be more sensible) re-invest it on their behalf in the product.

Local names and addresses of IFAs can be obtained from either of the following:

IFA Promotion Ltd., 17–19 Emery Road, Brislington, Bristol BS4 5PF. T:0117 971 1177.

The Money Management National Register of Fee-based Advisers, 172 Drury Lane, London WC2B 5QR. T:020 7074 1200.

Complaints

If you have a complaint about an IFA, the most likely person to be able to help is the PIA Ombudsman.

Before approaching him, you must first try to settle the dispute with the company or adviser direct. If this fails, the Ombudsman will investigate your complaint and if he finds it justified can award compensation. Although he has very wide powers, the Ombudsman cannot intervene over an actuarial dispute. Nor will he be able to assist if legal proceedings have been started.

For further information, write to the **PIA Ombudsman Bureau**, South Quay Plaza, 183 Marsh Wall, London E14 9SR. T:0845 080 1800.

N.B. In common with the Banking Ombudsman and others, the PIA Ombudsman is due to become part of the single Financial Ombudsman Service (FOS). You can contact either at the above address. For further information, see page 91.

Solicitors

Solicitors are professional advisers on subjects to do with the law or on matters that could have legal implications. They can assist with: the purchase or rental of property; drawing up a will; if you are charged with a criminal offence; or if you are sued in a civil matter.

Additionally, their advice can be invaluable in vetting any important document before you sign it. A solicitor can also help with the legal formalities of setting up a business; trusts; guardianship arrangements or other agreement, where the intention is to make it binding. Likewise, a solicitor would normally be the first person to consult if you were thinking of suing an individual or commercial organisation.

If you need to find a solicitor, often the best way is through recommendation. Your bank manager or accountant should be able to advise.

Alternatively, you could contact the **Law Society Records Department** on T:0870 606 6575, who will give you three names of solicitors in your area.

If you need financial as well as legal help, you could contact SIFA (Solicitors for Independent Financial Advice) which will send you details of up to six local firms able to advise about such matters as pension planning, investments or choosing a long term care policy. The address is: **SIFA**, 10 East Street, Epsom, Surrey KT17 1HH. T:01372 721172.

Community Legal Service Funding

The Legal Aid Board has been replaced by a new body called the Legal Services Commission. If you need a legal services solicitor (or want to find out if you are eligible for financial assistance), the place to go is your Citizens' Advice Bureau or other advice centre. Ask for leaflet *The Community Legal Service*, which will tell you about the different types of legal services which are available. There is a more detailed leaflet called *A Practical Guide to Community Legal Service Funding by the Legal Services Commission*. You can ask an adviser to go through this with you to help you work out if you are eligible. Leaflets about the services are also obtainable from many libraries or from the **LSC Leaflet Line**, St. Ives Direct, Enterprise Way, Edenbridge, Kent TN8 6HF. T:0845 3000 343.

Complaints

If you have a complaint against a solicitor, The Office for the Supervision of Solicitors (OSS) may be able to help. It can investigate such complaints as: failure to reply to letters; delay in dealing with your case; overcharging; wrongly retaining your papers; dishonesty and deception. It can also deal with complaints which allege 'inadequate professional service' (IPS) and is able to award compensation up to £5,000.

The OSS cannot, however, give legal advice or tell a solicitor how to handle a case; nor can it investigate claims of professional negligence. The difference between inadequate professional service (IPS) and negligence is that IPS is substandard work, whereas negligence is a mistake by your solicitor which has lost you money or caused some other loss for which you may be entitled to financial redress.

If you believe you have a complaint of negligence, the Office for the Supervision of Solicitors will either put you in touch with a solicitor specialising in negligence claims or refer you to the solicitor's insurers. If an appointment is arranged for you with a solicitor, he/she will see you free of charge for up to an hour.

For further information contact: **The Office for the Supervision of Solicitors**, Victoria Court, 8 Dormer Place, Leamington Spa CV32 5AE. Helpline: 0845 608 6565.

If you are still not satisfied, you can approach the **Legal Services Ombudsman** at Sunlight House, Quay Street, Manchester M3 3JZ. T: 0161 839 7262.

General queries. For queries of a more general nature, you should approach: **The Law Society**, 113 Chancery Lane, London WC2A 1PL. T:020 7242 1222.

For those in Scotland and Northern Ireland. If you live in Scotland or Northern Ireland, The Office for the Supervision of Solicitors will not be able to help you. Instead contact the Law Society at the relevant address below:

The Law Society of Scotland, The Law Society's Hall, 26 Drumsheugh Gardens, Edinburgh EH3 7YR. T:0131 226 7411.

The Law Society of Northern Ireland, Law Society House, 98 Victoria Street, Belfast BT1 3JZ. T:028 9023 1614.

Financial Ombudsman Service (FOS)

As from 1 December 2001, all the existing financial services ombudsman schemes and complaints handling organisations are due to be merged into a single Financial Ombudsman Service. Among others, this includes the Banking Ombudsman, the Insurance Ombudsman and the PIA Ombudsman. This will have the advantage of providing consumers with a 'one-stop' shop if they have a complaint about their dealings with a bank, building society, unit trust, OEIC, insurance company or independent financial adviser (IFA).

To all intents and purposes the FOS is already operating as if the merger had already taken place. As a result the FOS and individual ombudsman schemes can all be contacted at the same address and telephone number. If you are already dealing with a specific ombudsman, you should continue as you are. If not, contact the Financial Ombudsman Service at the following address: South Quay Plaza, 183 Marsh Wall, London E14 9SR. T:0845 080 1800.

7

Home Decisions

One of the most important decisions to be taken as you approach retirement is where you will live. To many people, one of the biggest attractions is the pleasure of moving home. No longer tied to an area within easy commuting distance of work, they can indulge their dreams of a cottage in the Cotswolds or a villa in some remote Spanish resort. While this could turn out to be everything they hoped for, and more, many people rush full steam ahead without any real assessment of the pros and cons.

Before you come to any definite decision, first ask yourself a few down-to-earth questions. What are your main priorities? To be closer to your family? To have a smaller, more manageable home that will be easier to run – and less expensive? To realise some capital in order to provide you with extra money for your retirement? To live in a specific town or village, which you know you like and where you have plenty of friends?

Or to enjoy the security of being in accommodation that offers some of the facilities you may want as you become older, such as a resident caretaker and the option of having some of your meals catered?

Staying put

While there may be plenty of arguments for moving there are probably just as many for staying where you are. Moving home can be a trau-matic experience at the best of times and even more so as you become older, when precious possessions are more painful to part with, as is usually the necessity when moving somewhere smaller.

Although ideally you may want to remain where you are, you may feel that your home is too large or inconvenient for you to manage in the future. Before rushing to put it on the market, it is worth consid-ering whether there are ways of adapting it to provide what you want. You might think about re-using the space in a better way. Would it be possible, for example, to convert a spare room into a work den and get rid of the clutter from the main living area? Have you thought about letting one or two rooms? As well as solving the problem of wasted space, it would also bring in some extra income.

A few improvements invested in now could make all the difference in terms of comfort and practicality. Many of us make do with inefficient heating systems that could be improved relatively easily and cheaply. Stairs need not necessarily be a problem, even when you are very much older, thanks to modern stair lifts. Even so, a few basic facilities installed on the ground floor could save your legs in years to come. Similarly, gardens can be replanned: extending the lawn or paving could spare you hours of exhausting weeding.

Moving to a new home

If you do decide to move, the sooner you start looking the better. With time to spare, you will have a greater choice of properties and more chance to weigh up the pros and cons.

While a smaller house will almost certainly be easier and cheaper to run, make sure it is not so small that you will feel cramped. When you are both at home, you may need more room to avoid getting on top of each other.

Also if your family lives some distance away, you may want the space to have them to stay.

If you are thinking of moving to a new neighbourhood, points to consider are: access to shops, proximity to friends, availability of public transport and whether the area offers the leisure facilities you enjoy.

Counting the cost

Moving house is expensive. It is estimated that the cost is between 5 and 10 per cent of the value of a new home, once you have totted up such extras as removal charges, insurance, stamp duty, VAT, legal fees and estate agents' commission. If you plan any repairs or decorations, the figure will be considerably higher.

A good tip to remember is that stamp duty (which applies to all properties costing more than £60,000) is not levied on fitments such as carpets and curtains. If you are considering a purchase which includes some of these, try to negotiate a separate price for them.

While on the subject of stamp duty, as you may know, there is now a higher rate on property purchases over £250,000. This was increased in the March 2000 budget from 2.5 to 3 per cent on properties costing over £250,000 and to 4 per cent on those costing above £500,000.

When buying a new home, it is essential to have a full building (structural) survey. This will cost around £400 for a small terraced house but is worth every penny. In particular, it will give you protection in law should things go wrong.

Bridging loans

Tempting as it may be to buy before you sell, unless you have the money to finance the cost of two homes – including possibly two mortgages – you need to do your sums very carefully indeed.

Banks usually charge 2 points or more over base rate plus an arrangement or administration fee on top. So, if bank rate is 6 per cent, the interest charged on a £100,000 loan works out at £666 a month; or £3,996 if it takes you six months to sell.

As an alternative to bridging loans, some estate agents may offer to buy your home at a discount. You would be 'selling on the cheap' and, while this could make sense, it is not a decision to be taken lightly.

Removal firms

Costs can vary considerably, so it pays to shop around and get at least three quotes. It is important to check exactly what you are paying for and whether the price includes packing and insurance.

A list of approved firms can be obtained from: **British Association of Removers**, 3 Churchill Court, 58 Station Road, North Harrow HA2 7SA. T:020 8861 3331 (please enclose sae).

Moving in with family or friends

There are many advantages to such an arrangement. While you are active, you can contribute to the household. Should you become frail or ill, help will be at hand.

Problems can also arise, however. As a precaution, try to work out in advance any potential conflicts. Questions to consider include: whether you will eat together; whether you will contribute in practical ways, like baby-sitting or shopping; also, whether you can keep a pet and have friends to stay.

Money is also a common source of dispute. Decide whether you will have your own telephone – or share one. If you will be paying rent, make it a formal arrangement exactly as if you were a normal tenant. You must agree a set figure: what it will cover, how it will be assessed in future and how it will be paid, i.e. weekly, monthly, cash or standing order. It is advisable to check with a solicitor or housing advice centre how sharing might affect your rights and obligations as either landlord or tenant. In particular, you should take advice before embarking on any construction work which might affect the property's exemption from capital gains tax in the future.

Retirement housing and sheltered accommodation

The term 'retirement' or 'sheltered accommodation' generally means property with a resident warden/caretaker, an emergency alarm system, optional meals and some communal facilities such as living rooms, garden and laundry. Guest accommodation and services such as hairdressers and chiropodists are sometimes also available.

Much of the property is run by local authorities, housing associations and charities. There are also many private developments, for sale or rent, at prices to suit most pockets. Some useful addresses are given in Chapter 11.

Making your home more practical

It is sensible to set about any home improvement plans earlier rather than later. For one thing, these are often easier to afford when you are still earning a regular salary. For another, any building work is tiresome and most people find it easier to put up with the mess when they are not living among it 24 hours a day. Thirdly, if you start early, you will enjoy the benefit that much sooner.

Insulation

Heat escapes from a building in four main ways: through the roof, walls, floor and through loose-fitting doors and windows. Insulation will not only cut the heat loss but will usually more than pay for itself within four or five years.

Loft insulation. Insulating materials are readily available from builders merchants. Or to employ a specialist, contact the **National Association of Loft Insulation Contractors**, PO Box 12, Haslemere, Surrey GU27 3AH. T:01428 654011.

Doors and windows. The two most effective ways of saving heat loss are double-glazing and draught-proofing. You could buy DIY products. Or if using a contractor, contact: **Glass and Glazing Federation**, 44–48 Borough High Street, London SE1 1XB. T:020 7403 7177;

Draught Proofing Advisory Association, PO Box 12, Haslemere, Surrey GU27 3AH. T:01428 654011.

Walls. More heat is lost through the walls than perhaps anywhere else in the house. Wall insulation (whether cavity or solid walls) is work for a specialist and, though expensive, should cut your heating bill by about a quarter.

For further information and addresses of registered contractors, contact:

Cavity Foam Bureau, PO Box 79, Oldbury, Warley, West Midlands B69 4PW. T:0121 544 4949.

Insulated Render & Cladding Association Ltd., PO Box 12, Haslemere, Surrey GU27 3AH. T:01428 654011 – for solid or defective walls.

Floor insulation. Up to 15 per cent of heat loss can be saved by filling cracks in the floorboards and skirting. Be careful not to block up the underfloor ventilation which protects floor timbers from dampness and rot.

Hot water cylinder insulation. You can save several pounds a week by insulating your hot water cylinder. Jacket should be at least 80mm thick and carry the BSI kitemark and BS 5615.

Heating

Your local gas and electricity showrooms, and also Solid Fuel Association, can advise on most matters to do with heating and hot water systems.

Buying and installing heating equipment. Faulty heating systems and slip-shod installations can kill. When buying equipment, check that it has been approved by the appropriate standards board.

For electrical equipment, the letters to look for are BEAB or CCA. For gas appliances, look for the CE mark. Domestic solid fuel equipment should be approved by the Solid Fuel Appliances Approval Scheme (see sales literature).

It is also essential to check that the contractor who installs your equipment is registered. The following organisations should be able to help with local names and addresses:

National Inspection Council for Electrical Installation Contracting, Vintage House, 37 Albert Embankment, London SE1 7UJ. T:020 7564 2323.

Electrical Contractors Association, 34 Palace Court, London W2 4HY. T:020 7313 4800.

Council for Registered Gas Installers, 1 Elmwood, Chineham Business Park, Crockford Lane, Basingstoke, Hants RG24 8WG. T:01256 372200.

Solid Fuel Association, Advisory Service (see local telephone directory).

Heating and Ventilating Contractors' Association, (for all types of central heating), ESCA House, 34 Palace Court, London W2 4JG. T:020 7313 4900; or call the **Home Heating Linkline** (all calls charged at local rate) on 0345 581158.

Energywatch, 6th Floor, Abford House, 15 Wilton Road, London SW1V 1LT. T:0645 060708. This is the statutory body representing gas and electricity consumers' interests in England, Scotland and Wales. If you have a problem which you cannot resolve with the supplier, contact your regional office (see back of your gas or electricity bill for address).

Tips for reducing your energy bills

Energy can be saved in lots of small ways. Taken together, they could amount to quite a large cut in your heating bills. You may find some of the following ideas worth considering:

- Set your central heating timer and thermostat to suit the weather. A saving of half an hour or one degree can be substantial.
- A separate thermostat on your hot water cylinder set at around 60 degrees Centigrade will enable you to keep hot water for taps at a lower temperature than for the heating system.
- If you run your hot water off an immersion heater, have a time-switch fitted attached to an Economy 7 meter so that the water is heated at the cheap rate overnight. An override switch will enable you to top up the heat during the day if necessary.
- Showers are more economical than baths as well as being easier to use when you become older.

- Reflective foil sheets put behind your radiators help to reduce heat loss through the walls.
- Switch off or reduce the heating in rooms not being used.
- An electric casserole is economical for single households. Pressure cookers and microwave ovens can save fuel and time.
- Finally, it is a good idea to get in the habit of reading your electricity and gas meters regularly. This will help you keep track of likely bills.

For a free Energy Efficiency Action Pack, telephone the **Energy Efficiency Hotline** on T:0845 727 7200.

Improvement and repair

Building work is notoriously expensive. It is worth investigating whether you could take advantage of some of the available grants.

Improvement and repair grants

Excepting certain items applicable to Disabled Facilities Grant, all grants are discretionary.

Renovation grant. There are seven main eventualities where application for a grant might be successful: (1) to bring a property up to a standard of fitness for human habitation; (2) for works to comply with a statutory repairs notice served on the owner; (3) to replace or repair rotten or defective parts of the structure including, for example, doors, windows, walls, an ineffective damp-proof course or unsatisfactory wiring; (4) for home insulation or other energy-saving work; (5) to provide heating facilities; (6) for the provision of satisfactory internal arrangements such as improvement of a very steep or winding staircase; (7) for conversions, such as the creation of a self-contained flat.

All claims for grant are at the discretion of the council. Eligibility is means-tested and different tests apply according to whether the applicant is an owner-occupier or tenant or whether he/she is a landlord. An individual's resources are taken into account in determining the actual amount of grant, so you could be required to contribute to the cost of the works.

The property must have been built or converted at least ten years before the date of application for grant. Second homes do not qualify.

Common parts grant. This is for the improvement or repair of the common parts of a building containing one or more flats. Items that normally count as 'common parts' include the roof, lift, staircase and entrance lobby. Grant can be applied for either by a landlord and/or by at least three-quarters of the occupying tenants. Tenants' financial resources are taken into account and (where applicable) the property must have been converted at least ten years previously.

HMO grant. This can only be applied for by a landlord and is for the improvement of Houses in Multiple Occupation; or for the conversion of a property for HMO use.

Disabled facilities grant. This is designed to adapt or provide facilities for a home (including the common parts) to make it more suitable for occupation by a disabled person. Grant can cover a wide range, including: work to facilitate access; the provision of suitable bathroom or kitchen facilities; the adaptation of heating or lighting controls; improvement of the heating system.

Provided the applicant is eligible, a mandatory grant of up to £20,000 may be available for all the above (councils may use their discretion to award more). Discretionary grant is also available for a variety of other works where these would make a home suitable for a disabled person.

The individual must be registered (or registrable) as disabled. There is a means test. The council will want to check that the proposed work is reasonable and practicable for the age/condition of the property and the social services department will need to be satisfied that the works are necessary and appropriate to meet the individual's needs. The grant can either be applied for by the disabled person or a joint owner/tenant or landlord, on their behalf. For further information, contact the Environmental Health or Grants Department.

Eligibility for all the above grants depends on the validity of the proposed work and on the applicant's resources, taking into account their income and any savings over £6,000.

Home repair assistance. HRA can help pay for small but essential works of repair, improvement or adaptation to your home, including works to make it suitable for an elderly or disabled person to come to live with you permanently.

Payment of the grant is at the discretion of your local council. Eligibility is restricted to those who are elderly, infirm or who are in receipt of one of the following: income support, housing benefit, council tax benefit, disabled person's tax credit, income-based jobseeker's allowance or working families tax credit. Applicants must normally either be an owner occupier or private sector tenant and the property itself must be their only, or main, home. People with a right to live in the dwelling for more than five years may be eligible if they have lived there for three years prior to making the application.

Maximum grant is £5,000 per application.

How to apply. Contact the Home Improvement Section or the Environmental Health Department of your local council for an application form.

Before making an application, you should read the DETR booklet on renovation grants (available from the council) which explains the requirements in detail and also suggests sources such as your Citizens' Advice Bureau that can help you assess your likelihood of qualifying and advise you of any preliminary steps (such as getting estimates) you need to take. Even if they are highly optimistic of your chances of obtaining a grant, **do not start work until approval has been given, as you will not be eligible for a grant once work has started**.

Community care grant. Income support recipients may be able to obtain a community care grant from the Social Fund to help with repairs. For further information, see BA leaflet GL18 *Social Fund*, obtainable from your local Social Security office.

Other help for disabled people

Your local authority may be able to help with the provision of certain special facilities such as a stair lift, telephone installations or a ramp to replace steps. Apply to your Social Services Department.

Useful reading

House Renovation Grants, Home Repair Assistance and Disabled Facilities Grant, obtainable from: DETR Free Literature, PO Box 236, Wetherby, West Yorkshire LS23 7NB.

Useful addresses

The British Wood Preserving and Damp-Proofing Association (BWPDA), 1 Gleneagles House, Vernon Gate, South Street, Derby DE1 1UP. T:01332 225100. Can advise on anything to do with wood preservation and damp-proofing in the home.

The Building Centre, 26 Store Street, London WC1E 7BT. T:020 7692 4000. Helpline (premium rate): 09065 161136. Displays a wide range of building products and appliances, has manufacturers' lists and can also advise about building problems.

Federation of Master Builders (FMB), Gordon Fisher House, 14–15 Great James Street, London WC1N 3DP. T:020 7242 7583. Lists of members are available from regional offices.

Guild of Master Craftsmen, Castle Place, 166 High Street, Lewes, East Sussex BN7 1XU. T:01273 478449. Can supply names of all types of specialist craftsmen.

Institute of Plumbing, 64 Station Lane, Hornchurch, Essex RM12 6NB. T:01708 472791. Can provide a list of professional plumbers; sae appreciated.

The Scottish and Northern Ireland Plumbing Employers' Federation, 2 Walker Street, Edinburgh EH3 7LB. T:0131 225 2255. Includes almost 1,000 plumbing and domestic heating firms. Lists of local members are available on request.

Royal Institute of British Architects, 66 Portland Place, London W1B 1AD. T:020 7580 5533. Has a free Clients' Advisory Service and can recommend suitable architects.

Royal Institution of Chartered Surveyors, The RICS Customer Services Department, Surveyor Court, Westwood Way, Coventry CV4 8JE. T:020 7222 7000. Can nominate qualified local surveyors.

Home Improvement Agencies

Home Improvement Agencies (sometimes known as Care and Repair or Staying Put projects) exist in many areas to help older or disabled house owners repair and adapt their homes. They will help to assess your needs, get a builder, supervise the work, raise the finance and check the completed job. Your Citizens' Advice Bureau should know about local schemes. Or you might usefully contact Anchor Trust which has 'Staying Put' projects across England: **Anchor Trust**, 7th Floor, Chancery House, St. Nicholas Way, Sutton, Surrey SM1 1JB. T:020 8652 1900.

Safety in the home

Accidents in the home account for 40 per cent of all fatal accidents. The vast majority are caused by carelessness or by danger spots in the home that for the most part could very easily be made safer.

Steps and stairs should be well lit and have a handrail along the wall to provide extra support. Frayed carpet on staircases should be repaired or replaced soonest.

Floors: rugs and mats can slip on polished floors and should always be laid on some form of non-slip backing material. Spilt water or talcum powder on tiled or linoleum floors is a number one cause of accidents.

The **bathroom** is another danger zone. Sensible precautionary measures include using a suction-type bath mat and putting handrails on the bath or alongside the shower. A bath seat can be helpful for older people. Soap on a rope is safer in a shower.

Fires can all too easily start in the home. If you have an open fire, you should always use a fireguard and sparkguard at night; and chimneys should be swept at least once a year. Upholstered furniture is a particular hazard. If buying new, make sure that it carries a red triangle label.

Portable heaters should be kept away from furniture and curtains and placed where you cannot trip over them. Paraffin heaters should be never be filled while alight. Avoid leaving paraffin where it will be exposed to heat; if possible, keep it in a metal container outside the house.

Gas appliances should be regularly serviced. Ensure there is adequate ventilation when using heaters. Never block up air vents: carbon monoxide fumes can kill.

A free safety check on gas appliances is available to anyone living alone who is over the age of 60 or registered disabled; or living with other people where everyone, like themselves, is either over 60 or registered disabled. To arrange a check contact your local British Gas office (see your last gas bill for telephone number).

More than one in three fires in the home are due to accidents with **cookers**. Pan handles should be turned away from the heat and positioned so you cannot knock them off the stove. If called to the door or telephone, always take the pan off the ring and turn off the heat.

Cigarettes left smouldering in a full ashtray could be dangerous. Smoking in bed is a potential killer!

Faulty **electric wiring** is another frequent cause of fires, as are overloaded power points. Wiring needs checking every five years and avoid using too many appliances off a single plug. (Ask an electrician's advice). Plugs should conform to British Standard 1363 and frayed or damaged flexes immediately replaced.

As a general precaution, keep **fire extinguishers** handy and make sure they are maintained in working order. Those above 1 kilo/1 litre need to conform to BS EN3; or, if made before 1996, to BS 5423. Small hand-held aerosol extinguishers should conform to BS 6165. Many insurance companies now recommend that you install a smoke alarm as an effective and cheap early warning device. Prices start from about £5.

Home security

The Crime Prevention Officer at your local police station will be glad to advise you how to improve your security arrangements.

The most vulnerable access points are doors and windows. Doors should have secure bolts or a five lever deadlock, strengthened by metal plates on both sides, a door chain and a spyhole. You might also consider outside lights to illuminate night-time visitors and an entry-phone so you can check who is at the door. Windows should ideally have key-operated locks that secure them when partially open; french windows need rack bolts or surface-mounted security pressbolts. You could also have window-bars and shutters.

Ensure the house is securely locked whenever you go out. Insist that official callers such as meter men show their identity cards before you allow them inside. If you are going away remember to cancel the milk and the newspapers. You might also consider using the Royal Mail's **Keepsafe** service for letters; ask at the post office.

For names of reputable locksmiths, contact: **Master Locksmiths Association**, 5d Great Central Way, Woodford Halse, Daventry, Northants NN11 3PZ. Freephone: 0800 783 1498.

Burglar alarms and safes

Many insurance companies will recommend suitable contractors to install burglar alarm equipment. Alternatively, contact: NACOSS, Queensgate House, 14 Cookham Road, Maidenhead, Berks SL6 8AJ, T:0870 205 0000.

If you keep valuables or money in the house, you should think about buying a concealed wall or floor safe.

Insurance

Seven out of ten householders are under-insured, some of them unknowingly but some intentionally to keep premiums lower. While understandable when money is tight, this has to be foolhardy. A better solution by far is to see whether you could obtain better terms than you are getting at present.

Some insurance companies offer home and contents policies for older people (age 50 and over) at substantially reduced rates. Among others, these can be arranged through: **Age Concern Insurance Services** (T:0845 606 5075) and **Saga Services Ltd**. (T:0800 414 525).

Many insurers also give discounts for installation of proper security precautions; some award extra points if the householder joins a Neighbourhood Watch Scheme. For names of brokers write to: **Institute of Insurance Brokers**, Higham Business Centre, Midland Road, Higham Ferrers, Northants NN10 8DW. T:01933 410003.

There are also appreciable savings with excess policies, i.e. where the householder pays the first chunk of any claim, say, the first £100 or £250.

Some people pay more than they need because they forget to cancel items which they have given away or sold. Equally, many forget to add new valuables they have bought or received as presents. You should also check that you are adequately covered for any home improvements you may have added.

An even more vital point is to ensure that your policy has not lapsed. If the insurance was originally arranged through your building society it may cease when your mortgage is paid off, in which case it will be essential for you to arrange new cover direct. Similarly, when buying for cash – for instance when moving to a smaller house – it will be up to you to organise the insurance and to calculate the rebuilding value of your home. It is advisable to get a qualified valuer to do this for you.

The **Association of British Insurers**, 51 Gresham Street, London EC2V 7HQ. T:020 7600 3333 will send you free information sheets on household insurance which describe what policies you need and indicate the correct amount of cover.

The **British Insurance Brokers Association**, BIBA House, 14 Bevis Marks, London EC3A 7NT. T:020 7623 9043, can send you a list of registered insurance brokers in your area.

Letting rooms in your home

Many people whose home has become too large are tempted by the idea of taking in tenants. For some, it is an ideal plan; for others, a disaster. At best, it could provide you with extra income and the possibility of pleasant company. At worst, you could be involved in a lengthy legal battle to regain possession of your property.

There are three broad choices: taking in paying guests or lodgers; letting part of your home as self-contained accommodation; or renting the whole house for a set period of time. In all cases for your own protection it is essential to have a written agreement and to take up bank references, unless the let is a strictly temporary one where the money is paid in advance. Otherwise, rent should be collected quarterly and you should arrange a hefty deposit to cover any damage.

To encourage more people to let out rooms in their home, the Government allows you to earn up to £4,250 a year free of tax. For further information, see Inland Revenue booklet IR 87 *Letting and Your Home*, available from any tax office.

Finally, if you have a mortgage or are a tenant yourself (even with a very long lease), confirm with your building society or landlord that you are entitled to sublet.

Paying guests or lodgers. This is the most informal arrangement with few legal formalities involved. Also as a resident owner, you are in a very strong position if you want your lodger to leave.

You would be wise to check with your insurance company about your home contents policy, as some insurers restrict cover to households with lodgers. Also, inform your lodger that his/her possessions are not covered by your policy.

Holiday lets. It is a good idea to register with your Tourist Information Centre and to contact the Environmental Health Office at your local council for any help and advice.

Useful reading

Want to Rent A Room? DETR leaflet, available from libraries, housing advice centres and Citizens' Advice Bureaux.

Letting part of your home. You could convert a basement or part of your house as a self-contained flat and let this either furnished or unfurnished.

Provided you continue to live in the house your tenant/s would have little security of tenure and equally would not have the right to appeal against rent. For further information, see DETR housing booklets *Notice That You Must Leave* and *Letting Rooms in Your Home,* available from CABs and local authority Housing Departments.

Tax note. If you later sell your home, you may not be able to claim exemption from capital gains tax on the increase in value of a flat if it is entirely self-contained. A solution is to retain some means of access to the main house or flat, but take legal advice as to what will qualify.

Renting out your home on a temporary basis. If you are thinking of spending the winter in the sun or are considering buying a retirement home for the future, you might be tempted by the idea of letting the whole house. For your protection you need to understand the assured shorthold tenancy rules; see DETR housing booklet *Assured and Assured Shorthold Tenancies: a Guide for Landlords*, available from your local housing department or from DETR Free Literature, T:0870 122 6236. It is strongly advisable to ask a solicitor to help you draw up the agreement.

Holiday lets

Buying a future retirement home in the country and renting it out as a holiday home is another option worth considering. As well as providing you with a weekend cottage at other times of the year, it can also prove a useful and profitable investment.

There are various attractive tax advantages which an accountant would explain. An important condition is that the property must be available for letting for at least 140 days during the tax year and be actually let for at least 70 days.

Housing benefit

Provided you have no more than £16,000 in capital or savings, you may be able to get help with your rent from your local council. You may qualify for housing benefit whether you are a council or private tenant or live in a hotel or hostel. The amount you get depends on: your income; your capital or savings; the number of people in your household; your eligible rent (up to a prescribed maximum); and your 'applicable amount', which is the amount of money the government considers you need for basic living expenses. At its most generous, benefit could be for the whole amount of your eligible rent.

Eligible rent. This includes rent and some service charges related to the accommodation but excludes meals, water rates and, as a rule, fuel costs. An amount will generally also be deducted for any adult 'non dependant' (including an elderly relative) living in your household.

Applicable amount. Your 'applicable amount' will generally be the same as the amount of income support for which you would be eligible. For details, see BA leaflet GL23, obtainable from your Social Security office.

How to claim. If you think you might be eligible for benefit (see BA leaflets GL16 and GL17), ask your council for an application form. The council should let you know within 14 days of receiving your completed application whether you are entitled to benefit and, if so, will inform you of the amount.

If you make a claim for Income Support you can claim housing benefit and council tax benefit at the same time. A claim form for these is included inside the income support claim form.

If you need any help or advice in understanding the forms, ask at your CAB or local Age Concern group.

Useful reading

Leaflet RR 2 *A Guide to Housing Benefit and Council Tax Benefit,* free from your council.

Council tax

Council tax is based on the value of the dwelling in which you live (the property element) and also a personal element – with discounts/exemptions applying to certain groups of people.

The property element. The value of the property is assessed according to a banding system, with eight different bands (A to H).

The valuation of each property is administered by the Inland Revenue Valuation Office. The ascribed value is based on prices applying at 1 April 1991. Small extensions/other improvements made after this date do not affect the valuation until the property changes hands. New homes are banded as if they had already been built and sold on 1 April 1991. If you think there has been a misunderstanding about the valuation (or your liability to pay the full amount) you may have the right of appeal. See 'appeals' further along.

Liability. Not everyone pays council tax. The bill is normally sent to the resident owner, or joint owners, of the property; or in the case of rented accommodation, to the tenant or joint tenants. Married couples and people with a shared legal interest in the property are jointly liable for the bill.

In some cases, for example in hostels or multi-occupied property, a non-resident landlord or owner will be liable but may pass on a share of the bill to the tenants/residents, which would probably be included as part of the rental charge.

The personal element. The valuation of each dwelling assumes two adults are resident. The charge does not increase if there are more adults. However if, as in many homes, there is just one adult, your council tax bill will be reduced by 25 per cent. Certain people are disregarded when determining the number of residents in a household.

There are also a number of other special discounts, or exemptions, as follows:

- People who are severely mentally impaired are disregarded; or, if they are the sole occupant of the dwelling, qualify for an exemption;
- Disabled people whose homes require adaptation may have their bill reduced to a lower band;
- People on income support should normally have nothing to pay, as their bill will be met in full by council tax benefit;
- Disabled people on higher rate attendance allowance need not count a full-time carer as an additional resident and therefore may continue to qualify for the 25 per cent single (adult) householder discount; exceptions are spouses/partners and parents of a disabled child under 18 who would normally be living with the disabled person and whose presence therefore would not be adding to the council tax;
- Young people over 18 but still at school are not counted when assessing the number of adults in a house;
- Students living in halls of residence, student hostels or similar are exempted; those living with a parent or other non-student adult are eligible for the 25 per cent personal discount;
- Service personnel living in barracks or married quarters will not receive any bill for council tax.

Discounts/exemptions applying to property

Certain property is either exempt from council tax or is eligible for a discount.

Discounts. Empty property (e.g. second homes) normally gets a 50 per cent discount. There are some exceptions – see below – where empty property is exempt.

Exemptions. The most common cases of exemptions include:

- Property which has been unoccupied and unfurnished for less than six months;
- Empty property in need of major repairs or undergoing structural alteration can be exempt from council tax for up to 12 months. After 12 months, the standard 50 per cent charge for empty properties will apply;
- Home of a deceased person: the exemption lasts until 6 months after the grant of probate;
- Home that is empty because the occupier is absent in order to care for someone else;
- Home of a person who is/would be exempted from council tax due to moving to a residential home, hospital or similar;
- Granny flats that are part of another private domestic dwelling may be exempt but this depends on access and other conditions. To check, contact your local Valuation Office.

Business-cum-domestic property

Business-cum-domestic property is rated according to usage, with the business section assessed for business rates and the domestic section for council tax. For example, where there is a flat over a shop, the value of the shop would not be included in the valuation for council tax. Likewise, a room in a house used for business purposes would be subject to business rates and not to council tax.

Appeals

If you become the new person responsible for paying the council tax on a property (e.g. because you have recently moved or because someone else paid the tax before) that you feel has been wrongly banded, you have six months to appeal and can request that the valuation be reconsidered. Otherwise, there are only three other circumstances in which you can appeal. These are: (1) if there has been a material increase or reduction in the property's value (2) if you start, or stop, using part of the property for business or the balance between domestic and business use changes (3) if either of the latter two apply and the listing officer has altered the council tax list without giving you a chance to put your side.

If you have grounds for appeal, you should take up the matter with the valuation office (see local telephone directory). If the matter is not resolved, you can then appeal to an independent valuation tribunal. For advice and further information, contact your local Citizens' Advice Bureau.

For further information, see leaflets: *Council Tax: A Guide to Your Bill* and *Council Tax: A Guide to Valuation, Banding and Appeals,* obtainable free from any council office or from DETR Free Literature, PO Box 236, Wetherby, West Yorkshire LS23 7NB.

Council tax benefit

If you cannot afford your council tax because you have a low income, you may be able to obtain council tax benefit. The help is more generous than many people realise. The amount you would get depends on: your income, savings, your personal circumstances, who else lives in your home (in particular whether they would be counted as a 'non-dependant') and on your net council tax bill. If you are not sure whether your income is low enough to qualify, it is worth claiming as you could be pleasantly surprised.

If you disagree with your council's decision, you can ask for this to be looked at again (a revision) or you can appeal to an independent appeal tribunal, administered by the Appeals Service. If you want a revision you should get on with the matter as soon as possible, as if you delay your request may be out of time.

For further information, ask your local Social Security office for BA leaflet GL17 *Help with Your Council Tax.*

Useful organisations

The following should be able to provide general advice about housing and help with housing problems:

- Local Authority Housing Departments
- Housing Advice or Housing Aid Centres
- Citizens' Advice Bureaux
- Local Authority Social Service Departments if your problem is linked to disability
- Welfare Rights Centres if your problem, for example, concerns a landlord who does not keep the property properly maintained
- Local councillors and MPs.

8

Leisure Activities to Enjoy

Whether you are looking forward to devoting more time to an existing interest, resuming an old hobby or trying your hand at something new, the choice is enormous.

The ideas in this chapter are just a small sample. Your library, local authority recreation department and adult education institute will be able to signpost you to other activities in your area.

While every effort has been made to ensure that prices are correct, those quoted should only be taken as a guide. The reason is that most organisations alter their charges from time to time and since there is no set date, it is impossible to keep track.

Adult education

Ever longed to take a degree, learn about computing, study art or do a language course? Opportunities abound with these and scores of other subjects available to everyone, regardless of age.

Adult Education Institutes

There is an Adult Education Institute in most areas. Classes normally start in September and run through the academic year. Many AEIs allow concessionary fees for students over 60. Ask your library for details. Or in London, buy *Floodlight* (£3.75), available from most bookstalls.

National Adult School Organisation (NASO), Riverton, 370 Humberstone Road, Leicester LE5 0SA. T:0116 253 8333. Promotes 'conversation with a purpose', through friendly discussion groups, meeting at places and times to suit their members. Social activities and conferences are organised nationally and regionally. Membership costs £10.50 a year. For further information, write to the above address.

National Extension College, The Michael Young Centre, Purbeck Road, Cambridge CB2 2HN. T:01223 400350. A choice of over 140 home study courses are listed in the NEC's free Guide, available on request. Cost is £80 upwards, with a discount for pensioners on the more expensive.

Open University, The Call Centre, PO Box 724, Walton Hall, Milton Keynes MK7 6ZS. T:01908 653231. Students are all ages – the oldest OU graduate was 92 – the majority of courses require no academic qualifications and there is a vast range of subjects from which to choose.

Courses normally involve a mix of: correspondence work, TV programmes, audio and video cassettes, contact with local tutors and, in some cases, also a residential school.

The Third Age Trust, University of the Third Age National Office, 26 Harrison Street, London WC1H 8JG. T:020 7837 8838. Offers a wide range of educational, creative and leisure activities. It operates through a national network of local U3As, which choose their own courses and social programmes according to members' interests. For a brochure, contact the address above enclosing sae.

Workers' Educational Association, Temple House, 17 Victoria Park Square, Bethnal Green, London E2 9PB. T:020 8983 1515. Offers a wide range of day and evening courses. Your library or education authority should be able to put you in touch with your local branch.

Arts

You can enjoy a glorious choice of events with many offering concessionary prices to retired people.

Regional arts boards

For first hand information about what is going on in your area, contact your regional arts board; or in the case of those living in Scotland, Wales and Northern Ireland, the national arts council. Most areas arrange an immensely varied programme with musical events, drama, arts and craft exhibitions and sometimes more unusual functions, offering something of interest to just about everyone. Many regional arts boards produce regular newsletters with details of events in their area. For addresses, ask at your local library.

Music and ballet

Scope ranges from becoming a Friend and supporting one of the famous 'Houses' such as Covent Garden to music-making in your own right.

Friends enjoy some very attractive advantages including in all cases priority for bookings.

Friends of Covent Garden, Royal Opera House, Covent Garden, London WC2E 9DD. T:020 7212 9412. Friends may attend talks, recitals, study days and 'open' rehearsals of ballet and opera. Annual membership is £55.

Friends of English National Opera, London Coliseum, St. Martin's Lane, London WC2N 4ES. T:020 7845 9420. Friends have the opportunity to apply for tickets for dress rehearsals and to gain an insight into the creation of opera through a variety of lunch-time and evening events. You also receive advance programme information. Membership for senior citizens costs from £25 a year.

Friends of Sadler's Wells, Sadler's Wells Theatre, Rosebery Avenue, London EC1R 4TN. T:020 7863 8198. Sadler's Wells has an ever-changing programme of ballet and contemporary dance. Friends receive free ticket offers and occasional invitations to talks and other events. Annual membership is £36.

Music making

Just about every kind of musical taste can be met. Information about local societies and other groups is contained in the *British Music Education Year Book* and the *British Music Year Book*, both of which should be in the reference section of your library.

Handbell Ringers of Great Britain, 87 The Woodfields, Sanderstead, South Croydon, Surrey CR2 0HJ. T:020 8651 2663. Arranges concerts, rallies, seminars and workshops. To contact your local group, write to the above address.

Making Music, 7–15 Rosebery Avenue, London EC1R 4SP. T:0870 872 3300. Can provide you with addresses of some 1,850 choral societies, orchestras and music societies throughout the country. Most charge a nominal membership fee and standards range from the semi-professional to the unashamedly amateur.

Society of Recorder Players, 15 Palliser Road, London W14 9EB. T:020 7385 7321. Players of all standards and ages are welcomed at the many branches. For list of addresses, please enclose sae. Annual subscription is £12. Branch membership varies.

Television and radio audiences

If you would like to be part of an invited studio audience, apply to the BBC through the relevant ticket unit for London-based programmes; or for outside London, through the appropriate regional centre. The ticket unit address for both radio and television is:

The Ticket Unit, **BBC Radio and Television Audience Services**, PO Box 3000, London W12 7RJ. T:020 8576 1227.

For independent television, audience participation is the responsibility of each programme maker and requests should be channelled to the contractor for the area.

Theatre

Theatre tickets need not cost a fortune! Preview performances are invariably cheaper and there are often concessionary rates for matinees. Herewith just a couple of places that offer special facilities of interest.

Barbican Centre, Silk Street, London EC2Y 8DS. T:020 7638 4141 (for information). Box office: 020 7638 8891. The Centre has two theatres, concert hall, art gallery, cinemas and library. There are often free live musical events and exhibitions. Pensioners can buy reduced tickets on a standby basis.

Royal National Theatre, South Bank, London SE1 9PX. T:020 7452 3000 (box office). Offers a host of attractive facilities as well as its three theatres. There are group price reductions and pensioners can buy matinee seats at £15. For membership details, contact Royal National Theatre, Mailing List, Freepost, London SE1 7BR.

Society of London Theatre (SOLT), 32 Rose Street, London WC2E 9ET. T:020 7557 6700. Senior citizens can get substantial reductions for midweek matinee performances at many West End theatres and also concessionary prices for other performances on a standby basis with all listings showing the symbol 'S' in the *London Theatre Guide*.

Concessions are subject to availability, so best check with the box office first. Senior citizens will need to show a travel pass or pension book as proof of their age.

The Society's *Disabled Access Guide to London West End Theatres* provides information about special facilities, access for wheelchairs and transport advice for disabled theatregoers. Available free from SOLT, T:020 7557 6751.

Leicester Square Ticket Booth. Sells tickets to many West End theatres at half-price on the day of performance. It is open to personal callers, Monday to Saturday from 10 a.m. – 7 p.m.; or in the case of matinees, until 1/2 hour before starting time. There is a service charge of £2.50 per ticket.

Late night trains. Late night trains, convenient for theatregoers, run from many London stations. For details of services, enquire at your local station or ring National Rail Enquiries on T:08457 48 49 50.

Visual arts

If you enjoy attending exhibitions and lectures, membership of some of the arts societies offers you a number of delightful privileges.

Contemporary Art Society, 17 Bloomsbury Square, London WC1A 2NG. T:020 7831 7311. Members can take part in an extensive programme of events including visits to artists' studios and parties at special exhibitions. Annual subscription is £30; £35 per couple.

National Art Collections Fund, Millais House, 7 Cromwell Place, London SW7 2JN. T:020 7225 4800. Members enjoy free admission to many museums and galleries plus a countrywide programme of lectures, private views and other special events. There are also art tours at home and abroad led by experts. Subscription is £30 a year; senior citizens, £22.

National Association of Decorative & Fine Arts Societies, NADFAS House, 8 Guilford Street, London WC1N 1DA. T:020 7430 0730. Events include lectures, museum and gallery visits, guided tours of historic houses and organised tours in the UK and abroad. Membership of a local society is about £20-£28 a year. Details are available from NADFAS, see above.

Royal Academy of Arts, Piccadilly, London W1J 0BD. T:020 7300 8000. Senior citizens enjoy reduced entrance charges to all exhibitions. Alternatively, you can become a Friend of the Royal Academy (£45) and enjoy free admission with an adult family member and four children under 16. Friends may also attend exhibition previews and use the Friends' Room to meet for coffee.

Tate Modern, Bankside, London SE1 9TG. T:020 7887 2000. London now boasts two magnificent Tate galleries: Tate Modern above and **Tate Britain** at Millbank, London SW1P 4RG. T:020 7887 8000. There are free weekly lectures and guided tours every day, except Sunday. Friends enjoy free admission to all exhibitions, receipt of *Tate: The Art Magazine* and access to Tate members' rooms. Basic membership is £24; or £36 for member plus guest.

Crafts

As well as being fun, proficiency in a craft is a means of beautifying your home – or can even develop into a flourishing cottage industry.

The Basketmakers' Association, Hon. Secretary: Mrs Isobel Edge, Highlanes Farm, Brockton, Eccleshall, Staffs ST21 6LY. T:01630 620363. Promotes the art of basketmaking, chair seating and allied crafts. It arranges courses, demonstrations and exhibitions. Membership costs £15.

Crafts Council, 44a Pentonville Road, Islington, London N1 9BY. T:020 7278 7700. The Crafts Council runs an information centre and reference library which can give advice on just about everything you could want to know: courses, addresses of craft guilds and societies, fact sheets on business practice as well as details of craft fairs and markets, galleries, shops and other outlets for work.

Embroiderers' Guild, Apartment 41, Hampton Court Palace, Surrey KT8 9AU. T:020 8943 1229. Members are offered a full programme of workshops, lectures, exhibitions and tours. They receive newsletters and a yearbook and can also join one of the 220 local branches. Full membership is £26.50; £17.50 for those over 60. Branches have their own subscription rates.

West Dean College, West Dean, Chichester, West Sussex PO18 0QZ. T:01243 811301. Organises short residential courses in the visual arts, crafts, photography, music and gardening. A typical programme includes: stained glass, calligraphy, textile design, woodcarving, black-smithing, jewellery and many more. Prices, which include full board, range from about £170 for a weekend to £405 for a five-day course.

Dance/keep fit

Clubs, classes and groups exist in all parts of the country, variously offering: ballroom, Old Tyme, Scottish, folk, ballet, disco dancing and others. There are also relaxation and keep-fit classes, many of which cater specially for older people.

The national organisations below can put you in touch with local groups. Your library and adult education centre should also be helpful.

The Central Council of Physical Recreation, Francis House, Francis Street, London SW1P 1DE. T:020 7854 8500. As well as infor-mation about sport, the CCPR can provide details of member organi-sations specialising in movement, dance and exercise, many of which have special sessions for over-50s. Contact the Marketing and Promotions Manager for Movement and Dance at the above address.

Imperial Society of Teachers of Dancing, Imperial House, 22–26 Paul Street, London EC2A 4QE. T:020 7377 1577. Can provide names of local teachers, many of whom organise classes especially for older people.

Keep Fit Association, Astra House, Suite 105, Arklow Road, New Cross, London SE14 6EB. T:020 8692 9566. The KFA offers 'Fitness through Movement, Exercise and Dance' classes, suitable for all ages and abilities. Almost all adult education centres run classes, many specially geared to keeping fit in retirement.

Royal Scottish Country Dance Society, 12 Coates Crescent, Edinburgh EH3 7AF. T:0131 225 3854. The Society has members from 16 to 80-plus in its many branches and groups all over the world.

For people with disabilities

Happily, there are increasingly fewer activities from which people with disabilities are debarred through lack of suitable facilities. This section deals with one topic not covered elsewhere, namely enjoyment of books.

Calibre, Cassette Library, Aylesbury, Bucks HP22 5XQ. T:01296 432339. Lends recorded books on standard cassettes to anyone with a doctor's certificate or other official form certifying their 'inability to read printed books in the normal way'. There are some 6,000 titles, including fiction and non-fiction.

National Library for the Blind, Far Cromwell Road, Bredbury, Stockport, Cheshire SK6 2SG. T:0161 355 2000. Lends books and music scores in Braille and Moon free of charge (also post-free).

RNIB Talking Book Service, Falcon Park, Neasden Lane, London NW10 1TB. T:020 8438 9000. This is a library service with more than 11,000 titles for anyone who cannot easily read normal print. The charge is normally paid by members' local authorities. Special recorder machines are available on permanent loan.

Games

Many local areas have their own bridge, chess, whist, dominoes, Scrabble and other groups who meet to enjoy friendly games. Your library should have details. Or, you can contact the national organisations below.

British Chess Federation, The Watch Oak, Chain Lane, Battle, East Sussex TN33 0YD. T:01424 775222.

English Bridge Union, Broadfields, Bicester Road, Aylesbury, Bucks HP19 8AG. T:01296 317200.

Scrabble Clubs UK, Mattel House, Vanwall Business Park, Vanwall Road, Maidenhead, Berks SL6 4UB. T:01628 500283.

Gardens and gardening

Gardens to visit, special help for people with disabilities, how to run a gardening association ... the organisations listed will be able to advise.

Gardening for the Disabled Trust & Garden Club, Hayes Farmhouse, Hayes Lane, Peasmarsh, Nr Rye, East Sussex TN31 6XR. Provides practical and financial help to disabled people who want to garden actively. The annual subscription is £4.

National Gardens Scheme, Hatchlands Park, East Clandon, Guildford GU4 7RT. T:01483 211535. (For England and Wales.) The Scheme covers some 3,500 private gardens which open to the public a few days a year to raise money for charity. Further information is given in the Scheme's Yellow Book, *Gardens of England and Wales Open for Charity* (£5 from booksellers). The organisation is always looking for suitable new gardens. Should you wish to offer yours, however small, apply to the county organiser (see handbook for address).

National Society of Allotment and Leisure Gardeners Ltd., O'Dell House, Hunters Road, Corby, Northants NN17 5JE. T:01536 266576. The Society encourages all forms of horticultural education and the forming of local allotment and gardening associations. Membership gives you access to free advice plus receipt of the Society's bulletin.

Royal Horticultural Society, PO Box 313, London SW1P 2PE. Members receive free entry to over 60 gardens and ticket discounts to RHS flower shows, including both Chelsea and Hampton Court Palace. They also receive a monthly copy of *The Garden* magazine plus free expert gardening advice. Membership costs £29 (plus a one-off enrolment fee of £7). For further information, telephone the Membership Department, on T:020 7821 3000.

Thrive, The Geoffrey Udall Centre, Beech Hill, Reading RG7 2AT. T:0118 988 5688. Offers support to those who no longer find gardening as easy as it once was, including for example information on where to obtain special tools.

History

People with an interest in the past have a truly glorious choice of activities to sample.

Age Exchange Reminiscence Centre, 11 Blackheath Village, Blackheath, London SE3 9LA. T:020 8318 9105. The Centre features exhibitions recording the life-styles of the 1920s and 1930s. There are also publications plus a year-round programme of activities including music and drama. Admission free.

City of London Information Centre, St. Paul's Churchyard (South side), London EC4M 8BX. T:020 7332 1456. The City of London offers enough interest to occupy you for a year or longer. The Centre gives advice and guidance and has lots of free leaflets.

English Heritage (Membership Department), Freepost WD 214, PO Box 570, Swindon, Wilts SN2 2UR. T:0870 333 1181. Manages over 400 historic attractions throughout England. Members enjoy free admission to all properties and receive a handbook, map and quarterly magazine. Annual subscription is £31; £20 for senior citizens.

Federation of Family History Societies, PO Box 2425, Coventry CV5 6YX. T:07041 492032. An umbrella organisation for more than 200 societies throughout the world (160 in the UK) that provide assistance if you are interested in tracing your ancestors. Write to the administrator, Maggie Loughram, enclosing (A4) sae.

Friends of Historic Scotland, Longmore House, Salisbury Place, Edinburgh EH9 1SH. T:0131 668 8999. Membership gives you free access to 330 historic buildings and ancient monuments, special guided tours and a quarterly magazine. Membership (2001) is £28 a year; £21 for over-60s; £31 for retired couples.

Historical Association, 59a Kennington Park Road, London SE11 4JH. T:020 7735 3901. Members enjoy a wide variety of activities such as lectures, conferences and conducted tours. There are over 70 local branches. Membership costs £30 a year; £19 for retired people.

Historic Houses Association (Membership), PO Box 21, Heritage House, Baldock, Herts SG7 5SH. Friends of the HHA enjoy free entrance to nearly 300 HHA-member houses and gardens and receive invitations to concerts, receptions and other events. Membership costs £28.

National Trust, 36 Queen Anne's Gate, London SW1H 9AS. T:0870 458 4000. Exists to protect historic buildings and areas of great natural beauty. Membership gives you free entry to the Trust's many properties. Hundreds of special events are arranged each year. Membership costs £31.

Hobbies

Most of the organisations listed arrange events, answer queries and can put you in contact with kindred spirits.

The British Association of Numismatic Societies, Secretary: P H Mernick, c/o General Services, 42 Campbell Road, London E3 4DT. T:020 8980 5672. An umbrella organisation for some 60 local clubs for those interested in the study or collection of coins.

British Jigsaw Puzzle Library, Clarendon, Parsonage Road, Herne Bay, Kent CT6 5TA. T:01227 742222. This is a lending library with puzzles usually exchanged by post. Subscriptions range from £30 for three months to £75 for a year. Postal charges are extra.

National Association of Flower Arrangement Societies, Osborne House, 12 Devonshire Square, London EC2M 4TE. T:020 7247 5567. Can put you in touch with local clubs and classes.

National Philatelic Society, 107 Charterhouse Street, London EC1M 6PT. T:020 7336 0882. Holds monthly Saturday meetings, usually including an auction. Members receive a journal and there is also an exchange packet scheme. Membership costs from £21 a year.

Museums

Most museums organise free lectures and guided tours. As with art galleries and theatres, an increasing trend is to form a group of 'Friends' who pay a membership subscription to support the museum and in return enjoy certain advantages, such as: access to private views, receptions and other social activities. Examples include:

British Museum Friends, The British Museum, London WC1B 3DG. T:020 7323 8605.

Friends of the Fitzwilliam Museum, Fitzwilliam Museum, Trumpington Street, Cambridge CB2 1RB. T:01223 332933.

Friends of the National Maritime Museum, Greenwich, London SE10 9NF. T:020 8312 6678/6638.

Friends of the National Museums of Scotland, Development Office, Chambers Street, Edinburgh EH1 1JF. T:0131 247 4191.

Friends of the V & A, Victoria and Albert Museum, Cromwell Road, London SW7 2RL. T:020 7942 2270.

Nature and conservation

The potential list is enormous. To give you a flavour, herewith a short 'mixed bag'. See also 'The Fun and Challenge of Voluntary Work' chapter.

Amenity organisations. You should be able to contact your local society through your public library.

The Civic Trust, 17 Carlton House Terrace, London SW1Y 5AW. T:020 7930 0914. Acts as an umbrella organisation for about 900 local amenity societies and publishes a quarterly newsletter with articles on planning, conservation and transport issues. Annual subscription is £20.

Forestry Commission, 231 Corstorphine Road, Edinburgh EH12 7AT. T:0131 334 0303. For information on walks, picnic places and visitor centres contact your local Forestry Commission office or the Public Enquiries service on T:0131 314 6322.

The Royal Society for the Protection of Birds, The Lodge, Sandy, Bedfordshire SG19 2DL. T:01767 680551. Acts to protect wild birds and the places in which they breed. Members enjoy free entry to 158 nature reserves. There is also a national network of local groups. Membership is £26; £35 joint.

The Wildlife Trusts, The Kiln, Waterside, Mather Road, Newark NG24 1WT. T:01636 677711. There are 46 local Wildlife Trusts caring for 2,300 nature reserves. If you would like to visit the reserves or participate in some of the many activities, such as joining a work party, contact your local Trust. Membership, which is optional, costs £20. For further information contact the above address.

Public library service

Britain's public library service is among the best in the world. It issues about 600 million books a year, loans records and cassettes and is a source of vast amount of information.

Many libraries have a mobile service and some also have volunteer library visitors who deliver books and materials to housebound people. Large print books are usually available as are musical scores, leaflets on DSS benefits, consumer information and details of local activities.

Sport

Retirement is an ideal time to get into trim. Facilities abound and, unlike people with a 9 to 5 job, you enjoy the great advantage of being able to book out of peak hours. To find out about opportunities in your area, contact your local authority recreational department.

Also useful to know about is: **The Central Council of Physical Recreation**, Francis House, Francis Street, London SW1P 1DE. T:020 7854 8500. Can give information and advice on all types of sport.

Angling

The Angling Trades Association, Federation House, National Agricultural Centre, Stoneleigh Park, Warwickshire CV8 2RF. T:024 7641 4999. Can advise on where to find qualified tuition, local tackle dealers and similar information.

Archery

Grand National Archery Society, Lilleshall National Sports Centre, Nr. Newport, Shropshire TF10 9AT. T: 01952 677888. Can put you in touch with your nearest club of which there are now over 1,200 around the country.

Badminton

Badminton Association of England Ltd., National Badminton Centre, Bradwell Road, Milton Keynes MK8 9LA. T:01908 268400. Most sports centres have badminton courts and give instruction, as do many Adult Education Institutes. If you need advice, or are interested in a short residential course contact the Association. Annual membership, which among other benefits includes physiotherapy insurance, costs (2001) £7.10 as a club member or £12.40 for non-club members.

Bowling

There are many clubs all over the country. For addresses contact:

English Bowling Association, Lyndhurst Road, Worthing, West Sussex BN11 2AZ. T:01903 820222.

English Women's Bowling Association, 2 Case Gardens, Seaton, Devon EX12 2AP. T:01297 21317.

English Indoor Bowling Association, David Cornwell House, Bowling Green, Leicester Road, Melton Mowbray, Leics LE13 0DA. T:01664 481900.

Clay Pigeon Shooting

Clay Pigeon Shooting Association, Bisley Camp, Brookwood, Woking, Surrey GU24 0NP. T:01483 485400. As a member you have public liability insurance, your scores are recorded in the national averages and you can compete in national events. Annual membership is £40; £30 for veterans (60 and over).

Cricket

Lord's Cricket Ground, St. John's Wood Road, London NW8 8QN. T:020 7432 1033. You can enjoy a conducted tour of Lord's. Price is £6.50 (£5 for pensioners). Tour times (normally noon and 2 p.m.) sometimes vary, so check before making a special visit. Half-price tickets are available to pensioners for some matches.

England and Wales Cricket Board, Lord's Cricket Ground, London NW8 8QZ. T:020 7432 1200. If you want to play, watch or help at cricket matches, contact your local club or send a sae to the above address.

Croquet

Croquet Association, Nigel Graves, Secretary, The Hurlingham Club, Ranelagh Gardens, London SW6 3PR. T:020 7736 3148. Many local authorities offer facilities for croquet enthusiasts. The Association runs coaching courses and can advise about clubs, membership and purchase of equipment.

Cycling

Cyclists' Touring Club, 69 Meadrow, Godalming, Surrey GU7 3HS. T:01483 417217. CTC offers members free third party insurance, free legal aid, a handbook, organised cycling holidays and introductions to 200 local cycling groups. Membership costs £25 a year; £15 for over-65s.

Darts

British Darts Organisation Ltd., 2 Pages Lane, Muswell Hill, London N10 1PS. T:020 8883 5544/5. Opportunities for playing darts can be found almost anywhere in clubs, pubs and sports centres. Contact the national body should you require further help.

Golf

English Golf Union, The National Golf Centre, The Broadway, Woodhall Spa, Lincs LN10 6PU. T:01526 354500.

Golfing Union of Ireland, Glencar House, 81 Eglinton Road, Donnybrook, Dublin 4. T:00 353 1 269 4111.

Scottish Golf Union, Scottish National Golf Centre, Drumoig, Leuchars, St. Andrews, Fife KY16 0DW. T:01382 549500.

Welsh Golfing Union, Catsash, Newport, Gwent NP18 1JQ. T:01633 430830.

The National Golf Unions can provide information about municipal courses and private clubs. Additionally many adult education institutes and sports centres run classes for beginners.

Rambling

Ramblers' Association, 2nd Floor, Camelford House, 87–90 Albert Embankment, London SE1 7TW. T:020 7339 8500. Will be glad to put you in touch with one of its many local groups. Membership is £20 a year; £11 for retired persons.

Swimming

Amateur Swimming Association, Unit 1, Kingfisher Enterprise Park, 50 Arthur Street, Redditch, Worcs B98 8LG. T:01527 514288. Classes are arranged by many authorities who also make the pool available at various times of the week for older people who prefer to swim quietly. The Association offers an award scheme as an incentive to swim regularly for fitness and health. Further details on request from the ASA.

Table Tennis

The Veterans English Table Tennis Society (VETTS), Harwood House, 90 Broadway, Letchworth, Herts SG6 3PH. T:01462 671191. Holds regional and national championships including singles and doubles events for over 40s, 50s, 60s and 70s. Annual membership is £10; £5 for those over 65.

Tennis

Veterans' Lawn Tennis Association of Great Britain, c/o Valerie Willoughby, 39 Molasses House, Plantation Wharf, London SW11 3TN. Promotes competitions for 'veterans' in various age groups. The VLTA Yearbook (£2) lists affiliated clubs as well as tournaments in Great Britain and Europe.

Yachting

Royal Yachting Association, RYA House, Romsey Road, Eastleigh, Hampshire SO50 9YA. T:023 8062 7400. There are 1,600 clubs affiliated to the RYA and more than 1,000 recognised teaching establishments. Membership costs £28 a year (£25 by direct debit).

Women's organisations

Although today women can participate in almost any activity on equal terms with men, women's clubs and organisations continue to enjoy enormous popularity. Among the best known are Women's Institutes, the Mothers' Union and Townswomen's Guilds.

Mothers' Union, 24 Tufton Street, London SW1P 3RB. T:020 7222 5533. The MU is an Anglican organisation. Members are involved in a wide range of projects within their local community and can attend branches for worship and fellowship.

National Association of Women's Clubs, 5 Vernon Rise, King's Cross Road, London WC1X 9EP. T:020 7837 1434. Typical activities include: crafts, keep fit, listening to guest speakers and outings to theatres and exhibitions. Membership is £6.50 a year to head office plus a small membership fee to the local club.

National Federation of Women's Institutes, 104 New Kings Road, London SW6 4LY. T:020 7371 9300. Through its community ties and wide-ranging activities, the WI offers women both friendship and the opportunity to develop their skills and talents. There is also a residential college, which runs short courses. Membership is £16.25 per annum.
   Women in Scotland and Northern Ireland should contact:

Scottish Women's Rural Institutes, 42 Heriot Row, Edinburgh EH3 6ES. T:0131 225 1724.

Federation of Women's Institutes of Northern Ireland, 209–211 Upper Lisburn Road, Belfast BT10 0LL. T:028 9030 1506.

Townswomen's Guilds, Chamber of Commerce House, 75 Harborne Road, Edgbaston, Birmingham B15 3DA. T:0121 456 3435. The Guilds have around 80,000 members who meet to exchange ideas, learn new skills and take part in a wide range of local activities. Annual subscription is £12.

Public Transport. One of the big gains of reaching retirement age is the availability of cheap travel. Most local authorities offer concessionary fares to senior citizens during the off-peak periods. Coaches too very often have special rates for older people and, as everyone knows, Senior Railcards, available to men and women over 60, offer wonderful savings.

9

The Fun and Challenge of Voluntary Work

Many people find immense satisfaction through becoming involved in some form of voluntary work. The choice of possibilities is enormous and your contribution will be greatly appreciated.

If you have a particular field of interest, such as children and young people or conservation work, you could find ideas by looking under the relevant heading further in the chapter. Alternatively, the following organisations will be able to advise, tell you what openings exist locally and point you in the right direction.

REACH, 89 Albert Embankment, London SE1 7TP. T:020 7582 6543. Specialises in placing men and women with management or other professional skills in voluntary organisations. All jobs are unpaid but with out-of-pocket expenses met.

Volunteer Bureaux. Most towns have a body of this kind which seeks to match volunteers with local organisations. For local addresses, see the *Volunteer Bureaux Directory,* available at most libraries.

Volunteer Development Scotland, 72 Murray Place, Stirling FK8 2BX. T:01786 479593. Can help you find out about volunteering opportunities by putting you in touch with a local organisation.

Wales Council for Voluntary Action, Baltic House, Mount Stuart Square, Cardiff Bay CF10 5FH. T:029 2043 1700. This is the umbrella body for voluntary activity in Wales. It can put you in contact with an organisation that would welcome your help.

Citizens' Advice Bureau. Your local CAB will also have information on local needs and groups to contact.

General

The scope of the work of the British Red Cross, WRVS and Citizens' Advice Bureau is so broad that they almost justify a category to themselves.

British Red Cross (BRCS), 9 Grosvenor Crescent, London SW1X 7EJ. T:020 7235 5454. The Red Cross needs help from men and women for first aid, vital community services, manning medical loan depots and fire victim support. Training is always given. Contact the local branch (under 'British' or 'Red Cross' in the telephone book) or write to the Volunteering Unit at the national headquarters above.

WRVS (Women's Royal Voluntary Service), Milton Hill House, Milton Hill, Steventon, Abingdon, Oxon OX13 6AD. T:01235 442900. The WRVS works in partnership with many organisations to cover a wide range of needs in the community. It particularly welcomes offers of help from men and women with time during the working day.

Activities include: meals on wheels, home support for elderly people, helping in hospital shops and assisting with welfare services in emergencies. No special qualifications are required, as training is given.

Citizens' Advice Bureaux deal with over 6 million enquiries a year. Apart from being an excellent source of information about other volunteer openings, the CAB itself has over 15,000 volunteer helpers working in its many branches throughout the country.

The work involves advising clients on a wide range of questions from welfare benefits to local community schemes. No formal qualifications are required but applicants must be able to master a considerable amount of detailed information.

Training is given and volunteers are expected to work a minimum of six hours a week in their Bureau. Contact the Manager of your nearest CAB for information.

Another organisation to know about is: **Community Service Volunteers (CSV)**, 237 Pentonville Road, London N1 9NJ. T:020 7643 6601. It operates a UK-wide programme called the Retired and Senior Volunteer Programme (RSVP) for people aged 50 and over who want to be involved in their community. Each local group plans its own activities which include befriending frail older people, helping children with reading and numeracy or working with health centres on care projects. Contact Denise Murphy, Director of RSVP.

Animals

Cinnamon Trust, Foundry House, Foundry Square, Hayle, Cornwall TR27 4HH. T:01736 757900. Seeks to help elderly pet owners who, owing to some emergency, are temporarily unable to care for their pets.

Animal lovers throughout the country assist either by fostering a pet in their own home or helping out on a daily basis, for example walking a dog or cleaning out a bird cage. Long-term homes are also required for pets who have lost their owners. For further details, write to Mrs. Averil Jarvis at the above address (enclosing sae).

Pet Fostering Service Scotland, PO Box 6, Callander FK17 8ZU. T:01383 730005. Provides a similar service in Scotland. If you have a love of pets and would like to help out in a crisis, telephone the above number.

Pets As Therapy, Rocky Bank, 6 New Road, Ditton, Maidstone, Kent ME20 6AD. T:01732 872222. Pets As Therapy is a national charity which originated the PAT visiting scheme to give those in hospitals and residential care homes the important contact with animals that many may miss. An essential is that the dogs/cats are fully vaccinated and well behaved. Annual subscription is from £10. If you would like to join, contact the above address.

Royal Society for the Prevention of Cruelty to Animals, Wilberforce Way, Southwater, Horsham, West Sussex RH13 7WN. T:0870 010 1181. Volunteers are needed to help with fund-raising. Contact headquarters for the address of your nearest branch.

Bereavement

Cruse Bereavement Care, Cruse House, 126 Sheen Road, Richmond, Surrey TW9 1UR. T:020 8940 4818. Cruse is the national organisation for people who have been bereaved. It provides counselling, practical help and organises friendship groups and drop-in centres. Volunteers are needed in the branches to help with all these services.

Children and young people

Action for Sick Children, 300 Kingston Road, Wimbledon Chase, London SW20 8LX. T:020 8542 4848. Local branches give practical help to sick children and their families including: providing transport to hospital; helping with volunteer play schemes on the wards and fund-raising to provide more parents' and children's facilities in hospital. Contact the HQ above for address of your local branch.

Barnardo's, Tanners Lane, Barkingside, Ilford, Essex IG6 1QG. T:020 8550 8822. Barnardo's provides many imaginative services for disadvantaged children. There are two ways you can help: by fund-raising (write to the National Volunteer Development Manager); and by supporting the Child Care Programme. This could involve helping a child with its reading or befriending a young person with a disability to give the mother a much-needed break (write to the Information Officer).

Children's Country Holidays Fund, 1st Floor (Rear), 42–43 Lower Marsh, Tanswell Street, London SE1 7RG. T:020 7928 6522. Contact: The Chief Executive. The purpose is to give disadvantaged London children a country holiday, either in private homes or camps. Host families are needed as are London organisers, camp supervisors and train marshals.

Save the Children, 17 Grove Lane, London SE5 8RD. T:020 7703 5400. This is an international charity working to create a better future for children. As well as fund-raising, helpers are needed to work in Save the Children shops, to assist with administrative tasks and to give talks to schools and church groups. Contact your local branch (see telephone directory) or call the Volunteer Actionline on T:0845 606 4027.

Scout Association, Gilwell Park, Bury Road, Chingford, London E4 7QW. T:0845 300 1818 . Volunteers are needed to help with: running weekly meetings, organising events, training (e.g. vehicle maintenance and map reading), editing newsletters and much else.

Sea Cadet Corps, 202 Lambeth Road, London SE1 7JF. T:020 7928 8978. Offers boys and girls aged 12–18 challenging new experiences and adventure. Units throughout the UK welcome volunteer help either as administrators or specialist instructors. Contact the national headquarters.

The Children's Society, Edward Rudolf House, Margery Street, London WC1X 0JL. T:020 7841 4400. It runs over 90 projects for highly vulnerable children and young people in England and Wales including giving practical support to those leaving care, excluded from school or in trouble with the law. Help is also needed in the Society's charity shops, as is fund-raising.

Volunteer Reading Help, 4th Floor, High Holborn House, 52/54 High Holborn, London WC1V 6RL. T:020 7404 6204. The purpose is to assist children aged 6 to 11 who need encouragement with their reading. Volunteers spare two hours, twice a week during term time, by going into a local school and giving individual attention to three children on a regular basis. No formal qualifications are needed but volunteers must have plenty of patience and be willing to commit themselves for at least a year. A short training is provided. For further information, if you would like to help, telephone the National Office above.

Conservation

BTCV, 36 St. Mary's Street, Wallingford, Oxfordshire OX10 0EU. T:01491 821600. Over 2,500 local groups run community projects including: planting trees, cleaning ponds, creating urban nature areas, restoring footpaths and protecting valuable habitats for wildlife. There is also a full programme of working holidays.

CPRE (Council for the Protection of Rural England), Warwick House, 25 Buckingham Palace Road, London SW1W 0PP. T:020 7976 6433. Volunteers act as local watchdogs, reporting unsightly development projects and threats to the environment and sometimes representing CPRE at enquiries. Fund-raising is also always needed.

Friends of the Earth, 26–28 Underwood Street, London N1 7JQ. T:020 7490 1555. Over 200 groups run local campaigns and fund-raising projects. These can be contacted through the London office where help with the administration is also much welcomed.

Greenpeace, Canonbury Villas, London N1 2PN. T:020 7865 8100. A pressure group which campaigns to protect the environment. Volunteers are needed both to help in the London office and also for campaigning by local groups across the country.

Ramblers' Association, 2nd Floor, Camelford House, 87–90 Albert Embankment, London SE1 7TW. T:020 7339 8500. Aims to keep footpaths open and to protect the countryside. Its 53 area offices need help with administration and with checking the condition of the local footpaths.

The elderly

Abbeyfield Society, 53 Victoria Street, St. Albans, Herts AL1 3UW. T:01727 857536. Builds houses to provide independent accommodation for older people who are on their own as well as residential care schemes for those who need a high degree of support. Volunteers assist in many ways: e.g. befriending residents, gardening, committee work, fund-raising or giving specialist legal/financial advice.

Age Concern England, Astral House, 1268 London Road, London SW16 4ER. T:020 8765 7200; **Age Concern Scotland**, 113 Rose Street, Edinburgh EH2 3DT, T:0131 220 3345; **Age Concern Cymru**, 4th Floor, 1 Cathedral Road, Cardiff CF1 9SD, T:029 2037 1566; **Age Concern Northern Ireland**, 3 Lower Crescent, Belfast BT7 1NR. T:028 9024 5729.

Age Concern promotes the welfare of older people. Local groups, using volunteer helpers, provide such services as day care, lunch clubs, home visiting and over-60s' clubs. For addresses, contact the national organisations listed above.

Carers UK, 20–25 Glasshouse Yard, London EC1A 4JT. T:020 7490 8818. Helps those who look after ill, frail or disabled people at home. It provides an advisory service and campaigns for a better deal for carers. Administrative help is needed at head office and at carers' groups, who meet to discuss mutual problems. Contact the above address for further details.

Contact the Elderly, 15 Henrietta Street, Covent Garden, London WC2E 8QH. Freephone: 0800 716543. Offers a way of making new friends and of providing companionship for lonely elderly people. Volunteers escort them once a month to enjoy tea in someone's home. Help is needed with driving (one Sunday a month) and/or hosting a tea-party for about 10 people once or twice a year. No expenses are paid. Ring the above number for name of local organiser.

Help the Aged, 207–221 Pentonville Road, London N1 9UZ. T:020 7278 1114. Provides funds for day centres, community transport, home safety devices, emergency alarm systems and sheltered housing.

Volunteer help is needed to staff charity shops and to assist local fundraising committees. Contact the Volunteer Co-ordinator.

The family

Marriage Care, Clitherow House, 1 Blythe Mews, Blythe Road, London W14 0NW. T:020 7371 1341. Runs pre-marriage courses and a counselling service for anyone with relationship problems. Help is needed in administering its 64 centres. New potential counsellors are also sought. For local addresses, contact the headquarters above.

Relate, Herbert Gray College, Little Church Street, Rugby, Warwickshire CV21 3AP. T:01788 573241. Volunteers who would like to become counsellors receive training. The work is most likely to appeal to people with some background in social or community activity.

SSAFA Forces Help, 19 Queen Elizabeth Street, London SE1 2LP. T:020 7403 8783. Volunteers deal with every kind of problem – domestic, financial, legal and compassionate. Training is given and although there is no minimum time commitment it is critical to see a case through to the end. Help is particularly needed in inner cities. A service background is not necessary.

Health and disability

British Ski Club for the Disabled, Hillingdon Ski Centre, Gatting Way, Park Road, Uxbridge, Middx UB8 1NR. T:01895 271104. Its aim is to encourage people with a disability to learn or continue to enjoy the fun of skiing and the self-confidence gained from participating in an exhilarating sport. Volunteers, who must be competent skiers, are needed to act as guides both on artificial slopes around the country and skiing holidays abroad. The Club runs its own guide courses. Small subsidies are available for guides on authorised holiday parties.

Calibre, Cassette Library, Aylesbury, Bucks HP22 5XQ. T:01296 432339. Volunteers are needed to help run the library and also to assist with publicity and fund-raising. Contact the Volunteer Co-ordinator, Sue Hawkes.

Cancer Research Campaign, 10 Cambridge Terrace, London NW1 4JL. T:020 7224 1333. Funds about one third of all cancer research carried out in the UK. Money for this is raised by local committees and through its 274 shops throughout the country. If you would like to help, see telephone directory for the address of your local group.

Imperial Cancer Research Fund, 61 Lincoln's Inn Fields, London WC2A 3PX. T:020 7242 0200. Carries out research into the causes, prevention and treatment of cancer. Help is needed in shops (sorting, serving, ironing, mending and similar), with fundraising and to assist with office work in the Regional Centres. See *Yellow Pages* for number of your nearest Centre or call the Volunteer Hotline on T:0845 076 0770.

Leonard Cheshire, 30 Millbank, London SW1P 4QD. T:020 7802 8200. Works with people affected by a wide range of disabilities, helping them to live their lives as they choose. Its many services throughout the UK are supported by local volunteers, who make a huge contribution.

There are endless practical ways you might help: driving, gardening, decorating, shopping and fund-raising. Contact the London office for the address of your nearest Cheshire service.

Mind (The Mental Health Charity), Granta House, 15–19 Broadway, London E15 4BQ. T:020 8522 1728 (for London); 0845 766 0163 (outside London). Works for a better life for people with experience of mental distress. The local associations (see telephone directory), vary in the scope of their work. While all will be involved in fund-raising, their activities also include running social clubs and day centres as well as giving support to individuals.

National Association of Hospital and Community Friends, 2nd Floor, Fairfax House, Causton Road, Colchester, Essex CO1 1RJ. T:01206 761227. Each League is autonomous and opportunities for voluntary work vary. All, however, are concerned with both service to patients and fund-raising. The National Association can put new volunteers in touch with their local League.

BackCare, 16 Elmtree Road, Teddington, Middlesex TW11 8ST. T:020 8977 5474. BackCare needs volunteers in their local branches to give practical help to back pain sufferers. Activities include: organising exercise and hydrotherapy classes, arranging talks and running social and fund-raising events. For further information, contact the Branches Officer.

Riding for the Disabled Association, Avenue R, National Agricultural Centre, Kenilworth, Warwickshire CV8 2LY. T:024 7669 6510. Provides opportunities for riding for disabled children and adults. You do not have to be horsey to help with the running of one of the 650 local groups. For those with experience of horses, the main jobs are leading or walking beside the ponies and accompanying parties on riding holidays. Contact the head office for address of your nearest group.

Royal National Institute for the Blind (RNIB), 224 Great Portland Street, London W1W 5AA. T:08457 669 999. RNIB aims to help blind and partially sighted people lead full and independent lives. Help is mostly required with fund-raising. Volunteers are also needed all over the country to service talking book players, two or three times a month. London office will put you in touch with your nearest group.

St. John Ambulance, 27 St. John's Lane, London EC1M 4BU. T:020 7324 4000. Best known for their first aid role at public events, St. John Ambulance volunteers also help with such activities as vehicle maintenance, fund-raising, public relations and community care. For information contact your county office or the national headquarters above.

SCOPE, Olympus House, Britannia Road, Patchway, Bristol BS34 5TA. T:0117 906 6309. Helpers are particularly needed for supporting one of the 250 local groups, helping in SCOPE shops and with fund-raising and street collections.

Sue Ryder Care, 114–118 Southampton Row, London WC1B 5AA. T:020 7400 0440. Their care centres cater for the sick and disabled of all ages. Volunteers are needed for a variety of jobs including help with the general running of the centres.

Heritage and the arts

Arts Council of England, 14 Great Peter Street, London SW1P 3NQ. T:020 7973 6517. There is attractive scope for becoming involved in the arts in a volunteer capacity. All kinds of abilities are needed from painting and other creative skills to accounting and clerical know-how. Ask at the library for the local address to contact.

National Trust, 33 Sheep Street, Cirencester, Glos GL7 1QW. T:01285 651818. Volunteers are involved in many aspects of the Trust's work in conserving the great houses open to the public as well as coast and countryside properties. Write to the Volunteers Office at the above address.

There is also a programme of working holidays in outdoor conservation. To obtain a brochure, telephone: 01603 739 543.

The needy

Elizabeth Finn Trust, 1 Derry Street, London W8 5HY. T:020 7369 6700. Assists people from professional or similar backgrounds either financially or with care in a number of residential homes. Work involves visiting patients and helping to organise outings for them; also fund-raising.

Oxfam, Oxfam House, 274 Banbury Road, Oxford OX2 7DZ. T:0845 300 0311. Volunteers help with the running of Oxfam shops, organise fund-raising events, give administrative help and support the educational aspect of Oxfam's work. For further information, contact your local Oxfam shop or office (see telephone directory) or write to the above address.

Royal British Legion, Poppy Appeal, Aylesford, Kent ME20 7NX. T:01622 717172. Best known for its Poppy Day Appeal, the Royal British Legion also runs care homes, maintains sheltered workshops, organises training, gives pension counselling and offers friendship through its many branches.

Its most pressing need is to recruit more Poppy Appeal organisers and volunteers for street, or house-to-house, collections. If you would like to help with the Appeal, contact the Head of the Poppy Appeal at the above address. If you would like to help in other ways, T:0345 725725.

The Samaritans, 10 The Grove, Slough, Berks SL1 1QP. T:08705 627282. The Samaritans offer emotional support to the suicidal and the despairing. Much of the work is done on the telephone and, while no special qualifications are required, an unshockable disposition and complete reliability are essential qualities in a volunteer. Training is given. The minimum time commitment is about 4 hours a week plus one night duty a month.

Work with ex-offenders

Nacro, 169 Clapham Road, London SW9 0PU. T:020 7582 6500. Opportunities for voluntary work are organised locally and include such projects as running activities for young people. For further details, contact the Resettlement Plus Helpline T:020 7540 6464.

Society of Voluntary Associates (SOVA), 1st Floor, Chichester House, 37 Brixton Road, London SW9 6DZ. T:020 7793 0404. SOVA trains volunteers to work alongside the Probation Service with offenders, their families and young people in trouble. The work may be with children, in the adult literacy scheme, prison visiting or helping ex-offenders. For further information, contact the above address.

10

Looking After Your Health

How often have you commented when meeting a recently retired friend: 'Goodness, he looks a different man. Fit, relaxed, contented – retirement must suit him.' And why not? Perhaps more than any other period since your twenties, retirement is a time for positive good health! You have more chance to be out in the fresh air and take up a favourite sport again. Also, once free of the strains and pressures that are part of any job, you will feel less harassed, look better and, best of all, have the energy to devote to new interests and activities.

Keeping fit

Exercise plays an important part in keeping you healthy. It tones up muscles, improves the circulation, reduces flab, helps ward off illnesses such as heart disease and, above all, can be a great deal of fun.

The experts' motto is: little and often. For those not accustomed to regular exercise, it is essential to build up gradually.

Training in a wide range of sports is available around the country – with many sessions especially focused on the over-fifties.

As well as some of the more exotic choices, swimming has long been recognised as one of the best forms of exercise. Some swear that there is nothing to beat a good brisk walk. Gardening is also recommended. With the explosion of leisure centres and keep fit classes run by local authorities, opportunities have never been better for athletes of all ability levels – and none.

Opportunities for more leisurely keep fit are also on the increase with plenty of options for older people. The town hall should be able to tell you what exists locally. The following organisations may also be able to help.

Extend, 22 Maltings Drive, Wheathampstead, Herts AL4 8QJ. T:01582 832760. Provides recreational movement sessions to music, especially for the over-sixties and people with disabilities. For information about classes in your area please enclose stamps to the value of £2.

The Fitness League, 52 London Street, Chertsey, Surrey KT16 8AJ. T:01932 564567. A national organisation that runs movement and exercise-to-music classes, with some participants aged 70 and older. Membership (including joining fee) is about £8. Classes cost from about £3 to £5.

Yoga

Around half a million people in Britain regularly practise yoga as a means of improving fitness and helping relaxation. Many local authorities run classes. Herewith also three specialist organisations which arrange courses in many parts of the country:

British Wheel of Yoga, 25 Jermyn Street, Sleaford, Lincs NG34 7RY. T:01529 306851.

Iyengar Yoga Institute, 223a Randolph Avenue, London W9 1NL. T:020 7624 3080.

Yoga for Health Foundation, Ickwell Bury, Biggleswade, Beds SG18 9EF. T:01767 627271.

Sensible eating

A trim, well kept body is one of the secrets of a youthful appearance, whereas being fat and out-of-condition adds years to anyone's age. Regular exercise is one-half of the equation, sensible eating the other. Not to put too fine a point on it, more than one in five adults in Britain is obese – in other words, overweight. No one is going to fuss about two or three pounds but half a stone or more, as well as looking unsightly, starts to become a health risk. In middle-aged men in particular, it increases the possibility of a heart attack, makes operations more difficult – and, in older people, is one of the causes of restricted mobility.

No one should go on a serious diet without first consulting their doctor. Medical advice is not necessary for knocking off: sweets, cakes, sticky buns, deep-fried foods, alcohol and rich sauces.

As a rule chubby people tend to be those who enjoy rather too many good meals in the company of others. People living on their own, however, sometimes also get weight problems: either because they cannot be bothered to cook for themselves, so snack off the wrong kinds of food such as jam sandwiches and chocolate biscuits; or because they neglect themselves and do not take enough nourishment. Elderly ladies, in particular, sometimes quite literally hardly eat enough to keep a bird alive and, in consequence, not only undermine their health but because of their general frailty are more susceptible to falls and broken bones.

Two excellent books for anyone living alone or for couples whose families have flown the nest are: *More Easy Cooking for One or Two* by Louise Davies, Penguin, £6.99 and *Quick and Easy Cooking for One* by Molly Perham, Foulsham £4.99

Food safety

No discussion about food would be complete without a word on the subject of food safety. As most readers will know it is inadvisable for anyone to eat uncooked dishes containing raw eggs. To be on the safe side, elderly people should probably also avoid lightly cooked eggs.

When it comes to risk of food poisoning, eggs are by no means the only culprits. 'Cook-chill' foods, including ready-cooked chickens and pork pies, are a breeding ground for bacteria especially in summer. Seafood too can be very dodgy in hot weather.

Storage and cooking play a major part in warding off sickness. The government leaflet *Food Safety* recommends the following basic advice:

- Keep all parts of your kitchen clean
- Aim to keep your refrigerator temperature at a maximum of 5oC
- Keep raw and cooked foods separate and use within the recommended dates
- Cook foods thoroughly
- Do not reheat food more than once and don't keep cooked food longer than two days.

Drink

Most doctors maintain that 'a little bit of what you fancy does you good'. Most healthy adults can enjoy a drink at a party or a glass of wine with dinner without any ill effects and retirement is no reason for giving up these pleasures. Moreover, in small quantities, it can be a very effective nightcap. Where problems begin is when people fancy more than is good for them. Alcoholism is the third great killer after heart disease and cancer.

The condition is far more likely among those who are bored or depressed and who drift into the habit of having a drink to cheer themselves up. The trouble is the habit can become insidious and individuals can quite quickly start becoming dependent on drink. The family doctor will be the first person to check with for medical advice. For those who need moral support, joining AA may be the answer.

Alcoholics Anonymous, PO Box 1, Stonebow House, Stonebow, York YO1 7NJ. T:01904 644026. Helpline: 0845 769 7555. There are over 3,000 groups around the country. Sufferers assist each other in coping which is made easier by meeting others with the same problem. Membership is free. For addresses of local groups, see telephone directory or contact the above helpline.

Smoking

Any age is a good one to give up smoking. The gruesome facts are that smokers are 20 times more likely to contract lung cancer. They are at more serious risk of suffering from heart disease and are more liable to chronic bronchitis as well as various other ailments.

Aids to will-power include: requesting a non-smoking table in restaurants; leaving your cigarettes behind when you go out; and refusing as a personal point of honour to cadge off friends. Working out how much money you would save and promising yourself a reward on the proceeds could help. Thinking about your health in years to come should be an even more convincing argument. Two organisations that offer support are:

Quitline, Victory House, 170 Tottenham Court Road, London W1P 0HA. T:0800 002200. Advice lines are open from 1 p.m. to 9 p.m., daily.

Smokeline (Scotland only), T:0800 848484. Available noon to midnight, seven days weekly.

Aches, pains and other abnormalities

Age in itself has nothing to do with the vast majority of ailments. However, many people ignore the warning signs when something is wrong, on the basis that this symptom or that is only to be expected as one becomes older. More often than not, treatment when a condition is still in its infancy can either cure it altogether or at least help to delay its advance.

The following should always be investigated by a doctor:

- any pain which lasts more than a few days
- lumps, however small
- dizziness or fainting
- chest pains, shortness of breath or palpitations
- persistent cough or hoarseness
- unusual bleeding from anywhere
- unnatural tiredness or headaches
- frequent indigestion
- unexplained weight loss.

Health insurance

Many people are covered by private health insurance or provident schemes during their working lives. If you wish to continue this benefit, most groups will be glad to welcome you as an individual client.

Even if you have not previously been insured, it is not too late to consider doing so. Although obviously this would be an extra cost, should you be unfortunate enough to fall ill or need an operation and want to be treated as a private patient, insurance will save you a great deal of worry and expense.

Terms and conditions vary but all the major groups offer to pay the greatest part of the costs of in-patient accommodation, treatment and medical fees as well as out-patient charges for specialists, X-rays and similar. However, policies do not normally cover GPs' costs. As with all types of insurance the small print matters, so make sure you understand exactly what you are being offered (likewise any exclusion clauses) before signing.

Organisations that offer private health insurance include:

Abbey National Healthcare. Details from any Abbey National branch or call T:0800 222399.

BCWA Healthcare, James Tudor House, 90 Victoria Street, Bristol BS1 6DF. T:0117 929 5555.

BUPA, BUPA House, 15–19 Bloomsbury Way, London WC1A 2BA. T:0800 600500.

Exeter Friendly Society, Lakeside House, Emperor Way, Exeter EX1 3FD. T:08080 556575.

Legal & General Healthcare, Freepost, PO Box 2344, Hove, East Sussex BN3 1BR. T:0500 669966.

Norwich Union Healthcare Ltd., Chilworth House, Hampshire Corporate Park, Templars Way, Eastleigh, Hants SO5 3RY. T:0800 142142.

PPP healthcare, Phillips House, Crescent Road, Tunbridge Wells, Kent TN1 2PL. T:0800 335555.

Royal Sun Alliance, Tamar House, St. Andrew's Cross, Plymouth PL1 1SG. T:0800 300990.

Saga Services Ltd., The Saga Building, Middelburg Square, Folkestone, Kent CT20 1AZ. T:01483 553553.

Standard Life Healthcare, Wey House, Farnham Road, Guildford, Surrey GU1 4XS. T:01483 440550.

Western Provident Association Ltd., Rivergate House, Blackbrook Park, Taunton, Somerset TA1 2PE. T:01823 623000.

If you would welcome advice in selecting a plan, you might like to contact **The Private Health Partnership.** They will send you a questionnaire and then help you match your key requirements to the most suitable scheme. There is a charge of £10 (plus VAT). For further information, telephone helpline: 01943 851133. You could also approach **Health and Group Bristol** which runs a telephone advice line and will send you details of plans most likely to suit your personal circumstances. T:0117 988 7533.

Private patients – without insurance cover

If you are not insured but want to go into hospital as a private patient, there is nothing to stop you doing so provided your doctor is willing and you are able to pay the bills. The choice is between the private wings of NHS hospitals, hospitals run by charitable or non-profit-making organisations and those run for profit by private companies.

Long-term care insurance

An emergency operation is one thing; long-term care because a person can no longer cope unaided, quite another. A number of insurance companies offer policies to help meet the costs of long-term care (e.g. nursing home or home care). These include: Scottish Widows, BUPA and PPP Lifetime Care.

N.B. Most such policies do not come cheap and the criteria for pay-out are normally pretty stringent. It is essential to ensure that you fully understand all the terms and conditions before signing. Best advice is to consult an independent financial adviser (IFA) for help. If you would like names of local IFAs with specialist knowledge of long term care, contact **IFACare Administration**, T:01299 406040.

Health screening

Prevention is better than cure and most of the provident associations offer a screening service to check general health. This is usually available to members of health insurance schemes and others alike.

National Health Service. The NHS offers several different screening services of particular relevance to those aged 50-plus. Two are specially for women and the others are more general.

All adults who have not been seen by a GP over the last three years can request to have a general check-up. This will include a few simple tests, such as checking your blood pressure, and the opportunity to discuss any health problems that could be worrying you. People over 75 should be offered an annual health check by their GP, which can either be done in their own home or at the practice premises. As well as general health, the check will cover such matters as eye sight, hearing, possible mobility problems, worries that may be causing depression and similar.

The special women's tests are to screen for cancer of the breast and cervical abnormalities. All women between 20 and 64 years are offered a smear test at least every five years; and all women between 50 and 64 years are invited for screening by breast X-ray every three years. (Women over 64 can request a breast x-ray every three years.)

You should automatically receive invitations for screening if you are registered with a GP. If not, ask your GP for details or enquire at your local health authority.

Hospital care cash plans

These schemes provide a cash sum for every night the insured person spends in hospital. Premiums start from £1 a week, giving a payment of about £18 a day. All benefits are tax-free and are available to anyone joining before age 65. About 28 organisations offer such schemes. A full list can be obtained from: **British Health Care Association**, 24a Main Street, Garforth, Leeds LS25 1AA. T:0113 232 0903.

National Health Service

Most readers will need no introduction to the National Health Service. However, there may be one or two scraps of information that you do not know that may come in useful around retirement.

Choosing a GP

If you move to a new area, you will need to find a new doctor. The best way is normally by recommendation; or you can enquire at your local Health Authority (HA), see telephone directory.

All GPs must now have practice leaflets, available at their premises, with details about the service. The information should include: names, addresses, sex, year of qualification and type of qualifications along with essential practice information such as surgery hours, services provided and arrangements for emergencies and night calls.

Having chosen a doctor, you should take your medical card to the receptionist to get your name registered. This is not automatic as, firstly, there is a limit to the number of patients any one doctor can accept. Also, some doctors prefer to meet potential patients before accepting them on their list. If you do not have a medical card, you will need to fill in a simple form.

If you want to change your GP, you go about it in exactly the same way. You do not need to give a reason for wanting to change and you do not need to ask anyone's permission.

Two useful publications to read are: *The NHS Reforms and You*; and *You and Your GP*. Available free from libraries, HAs and doctors' surgeries.

Help with NHS costs

Many people have an automatic right to free NHS prescriptions. These include: both men and women aged 60 and over; recipients of income support or income-based jobseeker's allowance; those suffering from a specified medical condition. The partner of anyone receiving income support or income-based jobseeker's allowance is also entitled to free NHS prescriptions.

Both also have a right to: free dental treatment, free sight test, NHS wigs, a voucher towards the cost of glasses and help with fares to hospital.

You may also be entitled to some help if you are in receipt of working families tax credit or disabled person's tax credit and are named on a current tax credit NHS exemption certificate.

Even if you do not qualify automatically, you may be entitled to some help on the grounds of low income. To find out, fill in claim form HC1 – obtainable from Social Security offices, NHS hospitals and many dentists, opticians and GPs – and send it to the address on the form. If eligible, then depending on your income, you will be sent either an HC2 (full help) or HC3 (partial help) certificate.

For further information about help with NHS costs, see leaflet HC 11 *Are You Entitled to Help with Health Costs?*

People under 60 who require a lot of prescriptions could save money by purchasing a 'prescription pre-payment certificate'. This costs £31.90 for four months; or £87.60 for a year. A prescription pre-payment certificate will work out cheaper if you are likely to need more than 5 prescription items in four months, or more than 14 items in twelve months. Obtain application form FP95 (EC95 in Scotland) from a post office, pharmacy or your Health Authority.

If you are on Income Support and have a disability, you may be entitled to certain premiums on top of your ordinary income support allowance. There are four rates: £22.60 (single); £32.25 (couple) for the generally disabled; and £41.55 (single and couples where only one is disabled) for the severely disabled; £83.10 if both are severely disabled.

Various Social Security benefits are also available to those with special problems because of illness. These include:

- *Incapacity Benefit*, see Leaflet IB 1
- *Attendance Allowance*, see Leaflet DS 702
- *Disability Living Allowance*, see Leaflet DS 704

All the above leaflets are obtainable from any Social Security office.

Going into hospital

Stories abound of people who wait months for an operation because of shortage of beds. But while waiting lists may stretch from here to eternity in one area, hospitals in another area may have spare capacity. Many patients are unaware that they can ask their doctor to refer them to a surgeon anywhere in Britain.

Finding out which hospitals have beds has become very easy. A **Government Health Information Service** has been established in each region which, among other information, can advise you which hospitals have the shortest waiting lists. Ring freephone: 0800 665544.

The **College of Health** operates a similar helpline, open 11 a.m. to 7 p.m., Monday – Thursday; and Friday, 11 a.m. to 5 p.m. T:020 8983 1133.

Before you can become a patient at another hospital, your GP will of course need to agree to your being referred.

Help is sometimes available to assist patients with their **travel costs** to and from hospital. If you receive income support or income-based jobseeker's allowance, you can ask for repayment of necessary travel costs. There are special schemes for people who live in the Isles of Scilly or the former Scottish Highlands and Islands Development Board area. Claims for help can also be made on the grounds of low income. See leaflet HC 11 *Are You Entitled to Help with Health Costs?*, available from Social Security offices and NHS hospitals.

If you go into hospital, you will continue to receive your State pension as normal for six weeks. After that, it will be reduced. See BA leaflet GL12 *Going Into Hospital?,* obtainable from any Social Security office.

If you have any complaints while in hospital, you should speak to the doctor or nurse or to the complaints manager; or if the matter is more serious, you should write to the Chief Executive of the hospital. If you are still unhappy, you can go to the Health Service Ombudsman – see addresses below.

If you are likely to need help on leaving hospital, ask to see the **Hospital Social Worker**.

Complaints

The NHS has a complaints procedure if you are unhappy about the treatment you have received.

In the first instance, you should speak to someone close to the cause of the problem, e.g. doctor, nurse, receptionist or practice manager. If you would prefer to speak to someone who was not involved in your care, you can speak to the 'Complaints Manager' at your local NHS Trust or Health Authority instead (for addresses, see telephone directory). In jargon terms, this first stage is known as **Local Resolution.**

If you are not satisfied with the reply you receive, you can ask the NHS Trust or health authority for an **Independent Review**. The Complaints Manager can tell you whom to contact.

If you are still dissatisfied after the Independent Review, then the Health Service Ombudsman (known formally as the Health Service Commissioner) might be able to help. He investigates complaints of failure or maladministration across the whole range of services provided by, or for, the NHS. He cannot, however, take up legal causes on a patient's behalf. Addresses to write to are:

Health Service Ombudsman for England, Millbank Tower, Millbank, London SW1P 4QP. T:020 7217 4051.

Health Service Ombudsman for Wales, 5th Floor, Capital Tower, Greyfriars Road, Cardiff CF10 3AG. T:0845 601 0987.

Health Service Ombudsman for Scotland, 28 Thistle Street, Edinburgh EH2 1EN. T:0845 601 0456.

If you have a complaint, you should get on to the matter fairly quickly. Time limits require you to register complaints within six months of the incident or within six months of your realising that you have reason for complaint (providing this is within twelve months of the incident itself). These time limits may be waived if you have a very good reason why you could not complain sooner.

If you need further advice on the complaints procedure, contact the Community Health Council or CAB.

You could also contact the **Patients Association**, PO Box 935, Harrow, Middx HA1 3YJ. Helpline: 0845 608 4455.

Eyes

It is advisable to have your eyes checked at least every two years. Eye tests are now free for all men, as well as women, aged 60 and over. If you are not yet 60, you can only get a free eye test if: you are registered blind or partially sighted; are prescribed complex lenses; are diagnosed as having diabetes or glaucoma; are over 40 and are a close relative of someone with glaucoma; or if you are a patient of the Hospital Eye Service.

You also qualify for a free sight test if you or your partner are getting income support or income-based jobseeker's allowance. You may also get some help if you are in receipt of working families tax credit or disabled person's tax credit.

Even if none of these apply but you have a low income, you may be entitled to some help towards the cost. Fill in claim form HC1, obtainable from Social Security offices, NHS hospitals and opticians. The Health Benefits Division will either send you a full help HC2 certificate; or an HC3 certificate which will state whether you are entitled to partial help – or have to pay the full cost yourself. Wait until you hear before having a sight test, as it is difficult to claim the money back afterwards.

The sight test should establish whether or not spectacles are needed. If they are, you will be given a prescription which is valid for two years. You are under no obligation to buy glasses from the optician who tested your eyes but can get them where you like.

There is a voucher system for helping with the purchase of glasses or contact lenses. If you or your partner are in receipt of income support or income-based jobseeker's allowance, you will receive a voucher worth between (2001/02) £30 and £154.30, depending on your optical prescription. For further details, see leaflets HC 11 *Are You Entitled to Help with Health Costs?* (available in large print size) and HC 12 *NHS Charges and Optical Voucher Values*, obtainable from main post offices, Social Security offices and NHS hospital. People who are registered blind are entitled to a special tax allowance of £1,450 a year.

For people with a more serious sight problem, a great deal of practical help, including special equipment, can be obtained by contacting the: **Royal National Institute for the Blind (RNIB)**, 224 Great Portland Street, London W1W 5AA, T:0845 766 9999.

All the main banks will provide statements in Braille at no extra charge. BT has a free directory enquiry service for blind and disabled customers. Call the free Linkline on: 0800 800150.

See also the 'Leisure Activities to Enjoy' chapter about libraries and other facilities.

Feet

Many people forget about their feet until they begin to give trouble. Corns and bunions if neglected can become extremely painful, and ideally everyone, especially women who wear high heels, should have chiropody treatment from early middle age or even younger.

Chiropody is available on the National Health Service without referral from a doctor being necessary but facilities tend to be very over-subscribed, so in many areas it is only the very elderly or those with a real problem who can get appointments.

Private chiropodists are listed in the *Yellow Pages*; or for names of local state registered practitioners, write to: **Society of Chiropodists and Podiatrists**, 1 Fellmongers Path, Tower Bridge Road, London SE1 3LY. T:020 7234 8620.

Hearing

Many people find their hearing begins to deteriorate as they get older. There are a variety of aids on the market that can make life easier. For example, BT has a range of special equipment from louder bell tones to flashing light systems. For information, dial BT free on 0800 800150. Hearing aids and batteries are free on the NHS.

The following organisations can give a lot of help and advice.

Hearing Concern, 7–11 Armstrong Road, London W3 7JL. Helpline: 0845 0744 600; (text) 020 8742 9151. Administers the Sympathetic Hearing Scheme and has local social clubs throughout the UK. Membership is £12.50 a year.

Royal National Institute for Deaf People, 19–23 Featherstone Street, London EC1Y 8SL. T:0808 808 0123; 0808 808 9000 (textphone). Publishes a comprehensive range of free leaflets. Membership including bi-monthly magazine is £16.50 a year; £10 for retired people.

British Deaf Association, 1–3 Worship Street, London EC2A 2AB. Tel/Text: 020 7588 3520. Works to protect the interests of deaf people and also provides an advice and advocacy service.

Teeth

Dentistry is one of the treatments for which you have to pay, unless you have a low income. Charges are based on 80 per cent of the cost up to a maximum of £360. If you or your partner are receiving Income Support or believe you may be entitled to reduced charges because your income is very low, get leaflet leaflet HC 11 *Are You Entitled to Help with Health Costs?*, together with claim form HC1 (from Social Security offices, main post offices and NHS dentists).

Personal relationships

Retirement is a bit like getting married again. It involves a new life style, fresh opportunities and inevitably, as with marriage, a few adjustments to make. He will have to get used to no longer going to a regular job. She will have to start thinking about another meal to prepare and may perhaps feel that she will have to reorganise her routine. It may, of course, be the other way round with the wife retiring later and the husband sighing at the prospect of a regular gourmet lunch to produce.

After years of perhaps hardly seeing each other for more than a few hours a week except for weekends, suddenly almost the whole of every day can be spent together. He may feel hurt that she does not appear more delighted. She may feel guilty about wishing to get on with her normal life. Even in the most loving marriages, the first weeks of retirement – for either partner – can produce tensions that neither had anticipated.

Normally with good will and understanding on both sides any difficulties are quickly resolved and an even deeper, more satisfying relationship develops. However, for some couples it does not work out so easily and it may be helpful to seek skilled guidance.

Relate, Herbert Gray College, Little Church Street, Rugby, Warwickshire CV21 3AP. T:01788 573241. Offers a counselling service to people who are experiencing difficulties in their marriage or other personal relationships.

Each counselling session costs about £25. No-one is turned away if they cannot afford to make a contribution. See local telephone directory under 'Relate' or 'Marriage Guidance' or contact the national headquarters above.

The address for Scotland is: **Couple Counselling Scotland**, 40 North Castle Street, Edinburgh EH2 3BN. T:0131 225 5006.

Similar services are offered by: **Marriage Care**, Clitherow House, 1 Blythe Mews, Blythe Road, London W14 0NW. Helpline: 0845 660 6000 (open Monday to Friday, 11 a.m. – 3 p.m.). **Scottish Marriage Care**, 196 Clyde Street, Glasgow G1 4JY. T:0141 204 1239. **Accord**, All Hallows College, Drumcondra, Dublin 9. T:00 353 1 837 5649; will be moving during 2002 to: St. Patrick's College, Maynooth, Co. Kildare.

Depression

Depression can be first cousin to marriage and other relationship problems. It is fairly common after bereavement, can be caused by worries or may occur after an operation. Sometimes too, as a number of retired people find, it develops as a result of loneliness, boredom or general lack of purpose.

Usually people come out of it of their own accord but if the condition persists a doctor should always be consulted, as depression can create sleeping difficulties and other problems. Another reason for seeing a doctor is that the symptoms may be due to being physically run down, as after 'flu, and all that is needed is a good tonic – or perhaps a holiday.

Sometimes, however, it may be that rather than medicines or the stimulus of a new activity, individuals may feel they need to talk to someone outside the family circle who has a deeper understanding of what they are experiencing.

The Samaritans, 10 The Grove, Slough, Berks SL1 1QP. T:08457 909090. The Samaritans are available at any time of the day or night, every single day of the year. They are there to talk or listen for as long as an individual wants. Although most people think of The Samaritans as being a service for those who feel they may be in danger of taking their own life, you do not need to feel positively suicidal to contact them. If you are simply depressed, they will equally welcome your call. The service is free and completely confidential. For your local branch, see in the telephone directory under 'S'.

Mind (The Mental Health Charity), Granta House, 15–19 Broadway, London E15 4BQ. Mind works for a better life for people with experience of mental distress. There are over 200 local associations, as well as day centres, social clubs, advocacy and self-help groups. Mind also publishes a large range of pamphlets and books. For further information, ring the Mind Infoline on: 020 8522 1728 (for London), 0845 766 0163 (outside London); or contact your local association (see telephone directory).

Some common afflictions

Quite probably you will be one of the lucky ones and the rest of this chapter will be of no further interest to you. It deals with some of the more common afflictions, such as back pain and heart disease. However, if you are unfortunate enough to be affected, or have a member of your family who is, then knowing which organisations can provide support could make all the difference in helping you to cope.

Arthritis and rheumatism

Arthritis Care, 18 Stephenson Way, London NW1 2HD. T:020 7380 6500. Has over 600 branches offering practical support including a visiting service, transport and social activities. Arthritis Care also provides specially adapted holiday centres. Publications subscription, including annual membership, is £18.

Arthritis Research Campaign, Freepost SF 671, PO Box 177, Chesterfield S41 7BR. T:01246 558033. Publishes a large number of free booklets on understanding and coping with arthritis. To receive information pack, please send 9" x 6" sae.

Back pain

Four out of five people suffer from back pain at some stage of their lives. While there are many different causes, doctors agree that much of the trouble could be avoided through correct posture, care in lifting heavy articles, a firm mattress and chairs that provide support in the right places.

The Back Shop, 14 New Cavendish Street, London W1M 7LJ. T:020 7935 9120. A shop and mail order business that sells medically approved products that help prevent back trouble or may provide relief for those who suffer. A free catalogue is available on request.

BackCare, 16 Elmtree Road, Teddington, Middlesex TW11 8ST. T:020 8977 5474. Funds research into the causes and treatment of back pain and publishes a range of free leaflets to help sufferers. Local branches organise talks, exercise classes and social activities. Membership is £17.50. Information packs are available at £3.

Cancer

One of the really excellent trends in recent years is a far greater willingness to talk about cancer. Quite apart from the fact that discussing the subject openly has removed some of the dread, increasingly one hears stories of people who have made a complete recovery. Early diagnosis can make a vital difference.

Anyone with a lump or swelling, however small, should waste no time in having it investigated by a doctor.

There are a number of excellent support groups for cancer sufferers. Rather than list them all, we have only included two as CancerBACUP, as well as its own services, can act as an information service about other local cancer support groups.

CancerBACUP, 3 Bath Place, Rivington Street, London EC2A 3JR. Freephone: 0808 800 1234. Offers a free and confidential telephone information service. Calls are answered by a qualified nurse who has the time, knowledge and understanding to answer your questions.

There is a regional centre in Nottingham (T:0115 840 2650); and another in Glasgow (T:0141 553 1553), where a face-to-face counselling service is offered. CancerBACUP also produces many booklets and factsheets on different types of cancer and their treatment. A publications list is available on request.

Breast Cancer Care, Kiln House, 210 New King's Road, London SW6 4NZ. Helpline: 0808 800 6000. Offers practical advice and emotional support to women with breast cancer including putting them in touch with others who have had a similar experience. It also offers a prosthesis fitting service.

Diabetes

Diabetes can be diagnosed at any age, although it is more common in the elderly and especially among individuals who are overweight.

Diabetes UK, 10 Queen Anne Street, London W1G 9LH. T:020 7323 1531. Offers information and support to all diabetics and their families. Around 450 local groups hold regular meetings and social activities. Annual membership costs £17 (£6 for pensioners and people on low income). For further details, contact the above address.

Migraine

Migraine affects over 6 million people in the UK. It can involve severe head pains, nausea, visual disturbances and in some cases temporary paralysis.

The Migraine Trust, 45 Great Ormond Street, London WC1N 3HZ. T:020 7831 4818. Offers a service to sufferers including helpline, free information pack, regular newsletters and local branches.

Osteoporosis and menopause problems

Osteoporosis is a disease affecting bones which become so fragile that they can break very easily. It affects one in three women (and also some men) and often develops following the menopause when body levels of oestrogen naturally decrease.

National Osteoporosis Society, Camerton, Bath BA2 0PJ. T:01761 471771. Offers support and advice on all aspects of osteoporosis. There is a medical helpline and also a network of over 120 local support groups. Membership, which is optional, is £10 and entitles you to free newsletters and publications.

Women's Health Concern (WHC), PO Box 2126, Marlow, Bucks SL7 2NB. T:01628 488065; Helpline: 01628 483612. WHC offers advice to women with gynaecological and hormonal disturbance problems, in particular with the menopause and proper use of HRT. It runs a telephone counselling service and also sees patients face-to-face at its centres in Newcastle, Surbiton, Blandford Forum, Birmingham and London. WHC charges no fee but donations are very much appreciated.

Stroke and heart disease

The earlier sections on smoking, diet, drink and exercise list some of the more pertinent, 'dos and don'ts' that can help prevent stroke and heart disease.

The Stroke Association, Stroke House, Whitecross Street, London EC1Y 8JJ. T:0845 303 3100. Provides an advisory service for stroke patients and their families. Home visits can be arranged and more than 400 Stroke clubs offer social and therapeutic support. For information contact the London office above.

Useful publications are also obtainable from the **British Heart Foundation**, 14 Fitzhardinge Street, London W1H 6DH. T:0870 600 6566.

AIDS

If you are concerned about the possibility of Aids and do not feel able to consult your doctor, there are a number of helpful organisations to which you can turn, including:

National Aids Helpline: 0800 567123. Free service, available 24-hours a day.

Terrence Higgins Trust Helpline: 020 7242 1010. Hours are 12 noon to 10 p.m. every day.

London Friend. T:020 7837 3337. This is a befriending and counselling agency for 'gay' and bi-sexual men and women. The helpline is open every evening between 7.30 p.m. and 10 p.m. London Friend also runs a number of social support groups.

GUM Clinics. Genito-urinary-medicine clinics exist in all NHS Hospitals. You can get telephone numbers from your local health authority. Or look in the telephone directory under 'Venereal' or 'Sexually transmitted diseases'.

Disability

Disability is mainly covered in Chapter 11, so if you or someone in your family has a problem, you may find the answer there. In this section, we list some of the key organisations that provide help.

Local authority services

Social Services Departments (Social Work Department in Scotland) provide many of the services which people with disabilities may need, including:

- Practical help in the home, perhaps with the support of a home help
- Adaptations to your home, such as a ramp for a wheelchair or other special equipment
- Meals on wheels
- Provision of day centres, clubs and similar
- Issue of orange badges for cars driven or used by people with a disability (in some authorities this is handled by the Works Department or by the Residents' Parking Department)
- Advice about other transport services or concessions that may be available locally.

A social worker will either make the arrangements or signpost you in the right direction.

Occupational therapists: can advise about special equipment and help teach someone with a disability through training and exercise how best to manage. Contact through the Social Services Department.

Health care

Services are normally arranged either through a GP or the local authority health centre. Key professional staff include:

- Health visitors: qualified nurses who, rather like social workers, will be able to put you in touch with whatever specialised services are required
- District nurses: will visit patients in their home
- Physiotherapists: use exercise and massage to help improve mobility, for example after an operation
- Medical social workers: employed at hospitals and will help with any arrangements before a patient is discharged.

Employment

The Disablement Resettlement Officer helps people looking for work and can also advise about any available grants, for example towards the cost of fares to work. Ask at your nearest Jobcentre.

Equipment

If you have temporary need of, say, a wheelchair, you will normally be able to borrow this from the hospital or local British Red Cross branch. If you want equipment including aids for the home on a more permanent basis, the best source of information is the Disabled Living Foundation Equipment Centre where all sorts of aids can be seen and tried out by visitors. Contact: **Disabled Living Foundation**, 380 Harrow Road, London W9 2HU. To check opening hours, which vary, T:020 7289 6111. For advice and information about equipment for daily living, telephone the Helpline on T:0845 130 9177.

If it is not possible for you to come to London, the **Disabled Living Centres Council** (T:0161 834 1044) will be able to recommend a centre nearer your home.

Another very useful organisation to contact for advice on equipment and home adaptations is RADAR – see below.

Finally, BT supplies many aids to enable people with disabilities to use the telephone more easily. For further information, dial BT free on 0800 800150.

Helpful organisations

Fount of all knowledge on almost every topic to do with disability is: **Royal Association for Disability and Rehabilitation (RADAR)**, 12 City Forum, 250 City Road, London EC1V 8AF. T:020 7250 3222; Minicom: 020 7250 4119.

It can give advice on: statutory and voluntary services, mobility issues, holidays, employment, the National Key Scheme for Toilets for

Disabled People (allows disabled people to use public loos when these would normally be locked against vandalism) and much else.

Motability, Customer Information Services, Goodman House, Station Approach, Harlow, Essex CM20 2ET. T:01279 635666. Aims to help recipients of the higher rate mobility component of disability living allowance, or war pensioners' disability allowance, get value for money when buying or hiring a car or buying a powered wheelchair. They can advise about special discounts and can sometimes give help in the form of a grant to meet costs that are not covered by the allowance.

Other useful addresses include:

Disability Wales/Anabledd Cymru, Wernddu Court, Caerphilly Business Park, Van Road, Caerphilly CF83 3ED. T:029 2088 7325.

Health Education Board for Scotland, Woodburn House, Canaan Lane, Edinburgh EH10 4SG. T:0131 536 5500.

Useful reading

Health and Well-Being: A Guide for Older People (HB6/96). Department of Health booklet, obtainable from Department of Health, PO Box 777, London SE1 6XH.

Disability Rights Handbook. Available from Disability Alliance, Universal House, 88–94 Wentworth Street, London E1 7SA. £12.50 (£8.50 for people in receipt of any benefit).

Health tips for travellers

If you are going abroad, it is essential to have proper medical insurance. Most experts recommend cover of £1 million for anywhere in the world.

Reciprocal arrangements for emergency treatment exist between Britain and other EC countries but facilities vary greatly both in quality and generosity. A Form E111 is a **must**. See Department of Health leaflet *Health Advice for Travellers* (T6) obtainable from any post office.

Other advice is plain common sense – but worth repeating for all that.

- Remember to pack any regular medicines you require: even familiar branded products can be difficult to obtain in some countries.
- Take a mini first aid kit, including: plaster, disinfectant, tummy pills and so on.

- If you are going to any under-developed country, consult your doctor as to what pills (and any special precautions) you should take.
- One of the most common ailments among British travellers abroad is an overdose of sun. In some countries, it really burns, so take it easy, wear a hat and apply plenty of protective lotion.
- The other big travellers' woe is 'Delhi belly', which unhappily can apply in most hot countries, including Italy and Spain. Beware the water, ice, salads, seafood, ice cream and any fruit which you do not peel yourself. Department of Health advice is only to eat freshly cooked food which is both thoroughly cooked and still piping hot. It is also advisable to check with your doctor.
- Always wash your hands before eating or handling food, particularly if you are camping or caravanning.
- Travelling is tiring and a sudden change of climate more debilitating than most of us admit: allow plenty of time during the first couple of days to acclimatise.
- Have any inoculations or vaccinations well in advance of your departure date.
- When flying, wear loose clothes and above all comfortable shoes as feet and ankles tend to swell in the air. To avoid risk of deep vein thrombosis, medical advice is to do foot exercises, walk around the plane from time to time, and to wear compression stockings, which can be bought from most chemists. On long journeys, it helps to drink plenty of fruit juice and remember the warning that 'an alcoholic drink in the air is worth two on the ground'. If you have a special diet, inform whoever makes your booking: most airlines, especially on long-distance journeys, serve vegetarian food.
- Finally, the old favourite, don't drink and drive.

Keep fit and have a wonderful holiday!

11

When Parents Need Extra Help

Most of us sooner or later have some responsibility for the care of elderly parents. While there is no hiding the fact that this can impose strains, most families cope exceedingly well.

Knowing what facilities are available, what precautions you can take against a mishap occurring and whom you can turn to in an emergency can make all the difference, both to you and to parents who may fear becoming a burden.

A basic choice for many families is whether parents should move in with them or continue to live on their own. While the decision will depend on individual circumstances, in the early days at least the majority choice is generally in favour of 'staying put'. Although later in the chapter we cover sheltered housing, an alternative solution to any move may be simply to adapt the home to make it safer and more convenient.

Ways of adapting a home

Many even quite elderly people will not require anything more complicated than a few general improvements, such as: better lighting, especially near staircases; a non-slip mat and grab-rail in the bathroom; safe heating arrangements; and perhaps the lowering of some kitchen and other units to place them within easy reach.

Another plan worth considering is to convert a downstairs room into a bedroom and bathroom, in case managing the stairs should later become a difficulty. These and other common-sense measures are discussed in Chapter 7.

For some people, however, such arrangements are not really suffi-cient. In the case of a physically disabled person, more radical improve-ments will usually be required. Far from presenting a major problem, today these are normally fairly easy to organise.

Local authority help

Local authorities have a legal duty to help people with disabilities and, depending on what is required and the individual's ability to pay, may assist with the cost.

Your parents can either approach their GP or contact the Social Services department. A doctor will be able to: advise what is needed; supply any prescriptions such as for a medical hoist; and can make a recommendation to the Housing Department, should rehousing be desirable.

The Social Services Department may be able to supply kitchen, bathroom and other aids for the home, arrange an appointment with an occupational therapist and support an application for a housing grant, should major adaptations be required.

Other sources of help

The Disabled Living Foundation, 380–384 Harrow Road, London W9 2HU. Helpline: 0845 130 9177; Minicom: 0870 603 9176. DLF runs an Equipment Centre, staffed by trained advisers, where aids of all kinds for the home can be tried out by visitors. For details of opening hours, which vary, telephone the above number.

The Royal Association for Disability and Rehabilitation (RADAR), 12 City Forum, 250 City Road, London EC1V 8AF. T:020 7250 3222. Can advise on almost all matters to do with disability and the home – plus just about every other topic where disability is an issue.

Both the **British Red Cross** and **Age Concern** (see local telephone directory) may loan equipment in the short term and be able to advise on local stockists.

Keep Able, Sterling Park, Pedmore Road, Brierley Hill, West Midlands DY5 1TB. A chain of specialist retail stores, stocking a wide range of gadgets to make life easier for disabled and elderly people. For further information, telephone the National Helpline on 08705 202122.

REMAP, Hazeldene, Ightham, Sevenoaks, Kent TN15 9AD. T:01732 883818. Can often help design or adapt goods to suit individuals, where there is no commercially available product to meet their particular needs.

The Centre for Accessible Environments, Nutmeg House, 60 Gainsford Street, London SE1 2NY. T:020 7357 8182. Runs an architectural advisory service and can recommend local architects with experience of designing for people with disabilities. When writing, you should give broad details of the type of work required.

Other helpful sources of advice include:

Disability Wales/Anabledd Cymru, Wernddu Court, Caerphilly Business Park, Van Road, Caerphilly CF83 3ED. T:029 2088 7325.

DIAL UK (National Association of Disablement Information and Advice Lines), St. Catherines, Tickhill Road, Doncaster DN4 8QN. T:01302 310123.

See also Housing Grants and Care and Repair in Chapter 7.

Alarm systems

It is worth thinking about alarm systems. The knowledge that help can be summoned very quickly in the event of an emergency can enable many elderly people to remain independent far longer than would otherwise be sensible. Some local authorities have alarm systems that can link people living in their own homes to a central control. Ask the Social Services Department.

Community alarms. Telephone alarm systems operated on the public telephone network can be used by anyone with a direct telephone line. The systems link into a 24-hour monitoring centre and have a pendant which enables help to be called even when the owner is some distance from the telephone. Grants may sometimes be available. One of the most widely used systems is SeniorLink, run by Help the Aged. For information, ring **SeniorLink Response Centre**, T:01709 389 388.

Commercial firms. For advice on choosing an alarm plus a list of suppliers, telephone **Disabled Living Foundation** on Helpline: 0845 130 9177.

Main local authority services

Local authorities supply a number of services which can prove invaluable to an elderly person. The two most important are meals on wheels and home helps. Social Services Departments have responsibility for assessing and co-ordinating arrangements for individuals according to their needs.

Meals on wheels

As you will know, the purpose is to deliver a hot lunch (or batch of frozen lunches) to people in their own home. In some areas, the scheme operates seven days a week; in others, only two or possibly less frequently, when frozen meals are supplied. Cost also varies: from about £1.50 to £2.50 a day, with the norm about £2. Contact the Social Services Department.

Home helps

Local authorities have a legal obligation to run a home help service to help frail and housebound elderly people with such basic chores as shopping, tidying up, a little light cooking and so on. The service is usually means-tested, so there may be a charge. Apply through the Social Services Department.

Specialist helpers

Local authorities employ a number of specialist helpers who are there to assist.

Social workers. Normally the first people to contact if you have a problem. They can put you in touch with the right person, if you require a home help, meals on wheels, have a housing difficulty or other query and are not sure whom to approach. You should ring the local Social Services Department; in Scotland, this is normally referred to as the Social Work Department.

Occupational therapists. Have a wide knowledge of disability and can assist a disabled person via training, exercise, or access to aids, equipment or adaptations to the home. Ring the Social Services Department.

Health visitors. Qualified nurses with broad knowledge both of health matters and of the various services available via the local authority. Rather like social workers, health visitors can put you in touch with whatever specialised facilities are required. Contact through the local Health Centre.

District nurses. Fully qualified nurses who will visit a patient in the home: change dressings, attend to other routine nursing matters, monitor progress and help with the arrangements if more specialised care is required. Contact through the Health Centre.

Physiotherapists. Use exercise and massage to help improve mobility and strengthen muscles, for example after an operation or to alleviate a crippling condition. Normally available at both hospitals and health centres.

Medical social workers. In the old days, used to be known as almoners. Are available to consult, if patients have any problems – whether practical or emotional – on leaving hospital. MSWs can advise on such matters as transport, after-care and other immediate arrangements. Work in hospitals and an appointment should be made before the patient is discharged.

Key voluntary organisations

Voluntary organisations complement the services provided by statutory health and social services in making life easier for elderly people living at home. The range of provision varies from area to area but can include:

- Lunch clubs
- Aids such as wheelchairs
- Good neighbour schemes
- Holidays and short-term placements
- Odd jobs and decorating
- Prescription collection
- Day centres and clubs
- Transport
- Advice and information
- Friendly visiting
- Gardening
- Family support schemes.

These services are not always provided by the same agency in every area. The CAB will advise you whom to contact. The following are the key agencies:

Age Concern may provide any or all of the services listed above. Most local groups recruit volunteers to do practical jobs and provide friendship. See local telephone directory.

Women's Royal Voluntary Service runs many local projects:

- Meals on wheels
- Lunch clubs
- Darby and Joan clubs
- Books-on-wheels
- Social transport
- Good neighbour scheme

See local phone book or contact the national headquarters: **Women's Royal Voluntary Service**, Milton Hill House, Milton Hill, Steventon, Abingdon, Oxon OX13 6AD. T:01235 442900.

British Red Cross also supplies some important services. The principal ones available from many branches include:

- Providing home-from-hospital support
- Helping sick, disabled or frail people make essential journeys
- Loaning medical equipment for short-term use at home and on holiday
- Respite for carers, such as for a planned short break or in an emergency if, for example, the carer falls ill
- 'Signposting' vulnerable people towards the statutory or voluntary services from which their needs may best be met.

To contact your local British Red Cross branch, see telephone directory, or write to: **British Red Cross (BRCS)**, 9 Grosvenor Crescent, London SW1X 7EJ. T:020 7235 5454.

St. John Ambulance volunteers help in hospitals and sometimes also assist people at home with, say, the shopping or by providing transport to and from hospital. In some areas loan of equipment such as wheelchairs, can be arranged. To get in touch, see local telephone directory or contact: **St. John Ambulance**, 27 St. John's Lane, London EC1M 4BU. T:020 7324 4000.

Other sources of help and advice

Civil Service Retirement Fellowship, 1b Deals Gateway, Blackheath Road, London SE10 8BW. T:020 8691 7411. Runs a home visiting service and organises a wide range of social activities for retired civil servants and their families through its many branches.

Counsel & Care, Twyman House, 16 Bonny Street, London NW1 9PG. T:0845 300 7585, open 10 a.m. – 12.30 p.m. and 2 p.m. – 4 p.m. Provides a free confidential advisory service, which is used by thousands of elderly people and their relatives each year.

SSAFA Forces Help, 19 Queen Elizabeth Street, London SE1 2LP. T:020 7403 8783. Provides whatever help may be needed to retired people who have served in HM Forces. This may typically include advice on pensions and benefits or the provision of a grant for a special need.

Jewish Care, 221 Golders Green Road, London NW11 9DQ. T:020 8922 2000. Provides services for elderly Jewish people in London and the South East, including domiciliary care, day centres plus some residential homes. Outside London, contact:

Leeds Jewish Welfare Board, 311 Stonegate Road, Leeds LS17 6AZ. T:0113 268 4211.

Manchester Jewish Community Care, 85 Middleton Road, Crumpsall, Manchester M8 4JY. T:0161 740 0111.

Brighton & Hove Jewish Welfare Board, 76 Marmion Road, Hove, East Sussex BN3 5FT. T:01273 722523.

Merseyside Jewish Community Care, Shifrin House, 433 Smithdown Road, Liverpool 15. T:0151 733 2292.

Transport

The difficulty of getting around is often a major problem for elderly people. In addition to the facilities run by voluntary organisations already mentioned, there are several other very useful services.

Voluntary and Community Schemes Database. Lists details of hundreds of transport schemes around the country and abroad, helpful to elderly and/or disabled people, including those needing to use a wheelchair. For further information, T:0845 758 5641 (voice and minicom).

Mobility Advice and Vehicle Information Service (MAVIS), O'Wing Macadam Avenue, Old Wokingham Road, Crowthorne, Berkshire RG45 6XD. T:01344 661000. MAVIS is an information service advising on all aspects of mobility – in particular, problems associated with driving. Its services include assessment of older motorists wishing to return to driving after a stroke or other disabling illness and advice on low-cost adaptations to relieve the pain of arthritic joints or other conditions that make driving uncomfortable. While general information is free, there is a charge for the more specialised services.

See also 'Disability Living Allowance', page 172.

Driving licence renewal at age 70

All drivers aged 70 are sent a licence renewal form and have to pay a £6 fee to have their licence renewed. The licence has to be renewed (and

£6 paid) at least every three years. Depending on their health and eyesight, the driver might be sent a new form after only one or two years. If this applies, the form must be completed honestly but no extra charge will be made.

Temporary living-in help and flexi care

Elderly people living alone can be more vulnerable to 'flu and other winter ailments. They may have a fall or, for no apparent reason, go through a period of being forgetful and neglecting themselves. In the event of an emergency, living-in help can be a godsend. Most agencies tend inevitably to be on the expensive side, although in a crisis often represent excellent value for money. Another longer-term possibility is to recruit a Community Service Volunteer.

Community Service Volunteers, 237 Pentonville Road, London N1 9NJ. T:020 7278 6601. Match full-time helpers with people who need a high degree of support. The volunteers, ages 16 to 35, are untrained and work for periods of 4 to 12 months. They provide companionship and practical assistance in the home.

Schemes are usually set up through a social worker, who supervises how the arrangement is working. There is an annual retainer of £2,100 (in case of real financial need, the local authority might pay) plus food and other allowances of about £59 a week. Contact the Social Services Department; or approach CSV direct.

Agencies. Both weekly charges and booking fees vary. Payment is normally gross, so your parents will not be involved in having to work out tax or national insurance. For a list of agencies, see *Yellow Pages* under heading 'Domestic' or 'Domestic Staff'.

A problem for many elderly people is that the amount of care they need is liable to vary according to their health and other factors including, for example, the availability of neighbours and family. Whereas after an operation the requirement may be for someone with basic nursing skills, a few weeks later the only need may be for someone to act as a companion – or simply to pop in for the odd hour during the day. An organisation well worth knowing about is:

United Kingdom Home Care Association, 42b Banstead Road, Carshalton Beeches, Surrey SM5 3NW. T:020 8288 1551. It represents over 1,000 agencies that specialise in providing care for older people.

All requirements are catered for including temporary and permanent posts, residential, daily, overnight and hourly work.

Nursing care

If one of your parents needs regular nursing care, their doctor may be able to arrange for a district nurse to visit them at home. This will not be a sleeping-in arrangement – simply a qualified nurse calling round when necessary.

If you want more concentrated home nursing you will have to go through a private agency. Many arrange hourly, daily or live-in nurses on a temporary or longer term basis. One of the best known, with 160 branches throughout the UK, is **BNA**, The Colonnades, Beaconsfield Close, Hatfield, Herts AL10 8YD. T:01707 263544. For branch addresses, call Freephone: 0800 657575.

Emergency care for pets

For many elderly people a pet is a most important part of their lives, providing companionship and fun as well as stimulating them into taking regular outdoor exercise. But in the event of the owner having to go into hospital or due to some other emergency being temporarily unable to care for their pet, there can be real problems including concern for the welfare of the animal and considerable distress to the owner.

To overcome these problems, two imaginative schemes have been set up, one operating throughout the UK and the other just in Scotland. Depending on what is required, volunteers will either simply feed or exercise the animal or will care for it in their own home until the owner can manage again.

Cinnamon Trust, Foundry House, Foundry Square, Hayle, Cornwall TR27 4HH. T:01736 757900. As well as the above services, Cinnamon also arranges permanent care for pets whose owners have died. Emergency services can be called 24 hours a day. The Trust makes no charge but donations, or a bequest, are very much appreciated.

Pet Fostering Service Scotland. T:01877 331496. The only charges are the cost of pet's food, litter – in the case of cats – and any veterinary fees that may be necessary.

Practical help for carers

If your parent is still reasonably active the difficulties may be fairly minimal. However, in the case of an ill or very frail person far more intensive care may be required.

If you go out to work, have other responsibilities or quite understandably feel that if you are to remain human you must have time for your own interests, it is important to know what help is available and how to obtain it.

The many services provided by local authorities and voluntary agencies, described earlier in the chapter, apply for the most part equally to an elderly person living with their family as to one living alone. If none of these solves your problems, ask your CAB or Social Services Department, as there may be some special local facility that could provide the solution.

In particular, you might ask about **day centres and clubs**. A responsible person will always be in charge and transport, to and from the venue, is often provided. Most areas also have **respite care facilities** to enable carers to take a break. This could be for just the odd day or longer, to allow carers who need it to have a real rest. Contact your Health or Social Services department.

Another service worth knowing about is **Crossroads**. It arranges for attendants to care for very frail or disabled people in their own home, while the regular carer is away. They will come in during the day, or stay overnight, as necessary. Priority is given to those in greatest need. Ask at the CAB or contact: **Crossroads**, Caring for Carers, 10 Regent Place, Rugby, Warwickshire CV21 2PN. T:01788 573653.

Holidays

There are various schemes to enable families with a dependent relative to go on holiday alone or simply to enjoy a respite from their caring responsibilities.

Some local authorities run **fostering schemes**, on similar lines to child fostering. Elderly people are invited to stay with a neighbour and live in the household as an ordinary family member. There may be a charge or the service may be run on a voluntary basis. Ask Social Services.

Some charities organise **holidays for older people** to give relatives a break. The Volunteer Bureau or Social Services should have details.

Another solution is a **short-stay home**, which is residential accommodation variously run by local authorities, voluntary agencies or private individuals. Again, Social Services should be able to advise.

If proper medical attention is necessary, consult your parent's GP. **Many hospitals and nursing homes** offer short-stay care as a means of relieving relatives and a doctor should be able to help organise this for you.

Fount of almost all knowledge on anything to do with caring is: **Carers UK**, 20–25 Glasshouse Yard, London EC1A 4JT. T:020 7490 8818 (general); 0808 808 7777 (CarersLine, Mon – Fri, 10 a.m. to noon; 2–4 p.m.) It has 120 self-help branches. Annual membership is £8, including receipt of the magazine *Caring*.

Useful reading

Caring for Someone?, free from Social Security offices.

Benefits and allowances

There are a number of benefits/allowances available to those with responsibility for the care of an elderly person and/or to elderly people themselves.

Entitlements for carers

Home responsibilities protection. A means of protecting your State pension if you are unable to work because of the need to care for an elderly person. See 'Understanding Your Pension' chapter (page 42) or ask any Social Security office for form CF 411.

Invalid care allowance. People who spend at least 35 hours a week looking after a severely disabled person (i.e. someone who gets Attendance Allowance, Constant Attendance Allowance or the two higher care components of Disability Living Allowance) may qualify for ICA. You do not need to live at the same address. The basic allowance is £41.75 a week (2001/02) and counts as taxable income. Carers who receive income support, housing benefit or council tax benefit are entitled to a special £24.40 premium.

Entitlements for elderly/disabled people

More generous income tax allowances. The personal allowance is increased when an individual becomes 65; and is raised again after their 75th birthday. The married couple's allowance is also increased when either partner reaches 75. Details of the increases, and how these are calculated, are explained in the Tax chapter, pages 47–49.

Attendance Allowance. This is paid to severely disabled people of 65 and over who have needed almost constant care for at least six months. Those who are terminally ill can receive the allowance without having to wait.

There are two different rates: £55.30 a week for those needing 24-hour care; and £37 for those needing intensive day or night care. The allowance is tax-free and is normally paid regardless of income. For further details and a claim form, get leaflet DS 702 from any Social Security office.

Disability Living Allowance (DLA). This benefit is paid to people up to the age of 65 who become disabled. It has two components – a mobility component and a care component. A person can be entitled to either one or to both components.

There are two rates for the mobility part of the allowance and three rates for the care component. More severely disabled people receive the higher amounts.

The (2001/02) rates for the mobility element are £38.65 and £14.65 a week.

The three rates for the care element are: £55.30; £37; and £14.65.

DLA is tax free and is paid regardless of income.

For further information get leaflet DS 704, from any post office, CAB or Social Security office.

Cold weather payments. These are designed to give particularly vulnerable people extra help with heating costs during very cold weather. Anyone aged 60 and over who gets Income Support or income-based Jobseeker's Allowance qualifies automatically. The amount paid is £8.50 a week and those eligible should receive it without having to claim. In the event of a problem, contact your local DSS office.

Winter fuel payments. This is a special annual tax-free payment of £200, given to all households with a resident aged 60 or older to help with the cost of winter fuel bills.

There is no need to claim, as all eligible persons should receive the payment automatically. For further information, ring the Winter Fuel Payment Helpline on T:08459 151515.

Free TV licence. People aged 75 and older no longer have to pay for their TV licence.

Financial assistance

A number of charities give financial assistance to elderly people in need. Most have particular criteria such as, for example, a service background, disability, religion or other. To find out which would be worth approaching, ask your library for: *A Guide to Grants for Individuals in Need*, published by the Directory of Social Change; also *The Charities Digest*, published by Waterlow Professional Publishing.

Special accommodation

Retired people who need particular support may choose or need to move to accommodation where special services are provided. This can either be sheltered housing or a residential home. Both terms cover an enormous spectrum, so anyone considering either of these options should make a point of investigating thoroughly before reaching a decision.

Sheltered housing

Sheltered housing is usually a development of purpose-designed bungalows or flats within easy access of shops and public transport. They generally have a warden, an alarm system and some common facilities, such as: a garden, launderette and a dining room where meals are provided, on an optional basis, either once a day or several days a week.

Sheltered housing is available for sale or rental, variously through private developers, housing associations or local authorities.

Sheltered housing for sale

Flats and houses are normally sold on long leases (99 years or more). Should a resident decide to move, the property can usually be sold on the open market, provided the prospective buyer is over 55 years of age. Most developers impose a levy of 1 per cent of the sale price for checking the credentials of incoming residents. Look carefully at any schemes that enable you to buy the property at a discount as some entitle the developer to retain part of the equity on resale.

There will be a weekly or monthly service charge and residents normally have to enter into a management agreement with the housebuilder. It is important to be sure exactly what the commitment is before buying. Factors to check include: who the managing agent is;

the warden's duties; what the service charge covers; the ground rent; the arrangements for any repairs that might be necessary; whether there is a residents' association; whether pets are allowed; what the conditions are with regard to reselling the property – and the tenant's rights in the matter.

Prices range from approximately £40,000 to £450,000 – depending on size, location and type of property. Weekly service charges vary between roughly £35 and £55, with around £40 being the norm.

The service charge usually covers: the cost of the warden, alarm system, maintenance, repair and renewal of any communal facilities (external and internal) and sometimes the heating and lighting costs. It may also cover insurance on the building (but not the contents). Be wary of service charges that seem uncommonly reasonable, as these are often increased well above inflation following purchase.

Those on lowish incomes may be able to get housing benefit to meet some or all of the service charge. For advice, ask at the Housing Department.

The following organisations can provide information about sheltered housing for sale:

AIM, Walkden House, 3–10 Melton Street, London NW1 2EB. T:020 7383 2006. Offers information, legal advice and a mediation service to residents of both rented sheltered housing and private retirement housing.

Elderly Accommodation Counsel, 3rd Floor, 89 Albert Embankment, London SE1 7TP. T:020 7820 1343. Maintains a nationwide database of all types of accommodation for older people and gives advice and information to help individuals choose the accommodation most suited to their needs.

Rented sheltered housing

This is normally provided by local authorities, housing associations and certain benevolent societies. As with accommodation to buy, quality varies.

Local authorities. This is usually only available to local residents. There is often a minimum/maximum age and applicants may be asked to have a medical examination. Apply to the local Housing or Social Services Department.

Housing associations. Supply much of the newly built sheltered housing. Rents, which sometimes include service charge, vary very roughly from £50 to £95 a week.

Some charitable housing associations, offer a licensee arrangement which does not provide the same security of tenure as other tenancy agreements. You are strongly advised to have the proposed contract checked by a lawyer before signing it.

CABs and Housing Departments often keep a list of local housing associations. Otherwise contact: **Housing Corporation**, 149 Tottenham Court Road, London W1T 7BN. T:020 7393 2000.

For Scotland, Wales and Northern Ireland, contact:

The Housing Department of the Welsh Office, Cathay Park, Cardiff CF10 3NQ. T:029 2082 5111.

Scottish Homes, Thistle House, 91 Haymarket Terrace, Edinburgh EH12 5HE. T:0131 313 0044.

Northern Ireland Housing Executive, The Housing Centre, 2 Adelaide Street, Belfast BT2 8PB. T:028 9024 0588.

Benevolent societies. These all cater for specific professional and other groups, for example: SSAFA Forces Help and TBF: The Teacher Support Network.

Almshouses

This is sheltered housing for elderly people of reduced means, which is administered by a charitable trust. Rents are not charged but there may be a maintenance contribution towards upkeep and heating. For further information, write to: **The Almshouse Association**, Billingbear Lodge, Wokingham, Berkshire RG40 5RU. T:01344 452922.

Community care

Anyone needing help in arranging suitable care for an elderly person should contact their local Social Services department. They will assess what type of provision would best meet the needs of the individual. This could be either services or special equipment to enable them to stay in their own home; residential home accommodation; or a nursing home. If residential or nursing home care is necessary, the department will arrange a place, pay the charge and seek reimbursement according to the person's means. (See 'Financial Assistance for Residential and Nursing Home Care', page 177).

Residential care homes

The accommodation usually consists of a bedroom plus communal dining rooms, lounges and gardens. All meals are provided, rooms are cleaned and staff are at hand to give whatever help is needed. Most homes are fully furnished, though it is usually possible to take small items of furniture. Except in some of the more expensive private homes, bathrooms are normally shared.

Homes are run by private individuals (or companies), voluntary organisations and local authorities. All private and voluntary homes should be registered with the Social Services to ensure minimum standards. No home should ever be accepted 'on spec'. It is very important that the person should have a proper chance to visit it and ask any questions.

Private homes. Private rest homes tend to be smaller than those run by councils, taking up to about 30 people. Fees cover an enormous range, from about £250 to £750 a week, or even more.

Voluntary rest homes. These are run by charities, religious bodies or other voluntary organisations. Eligibility may be determined by age, background, occupation or general fitness. Fees range from about £250 to £550 a week – and even higher for Greater London.

Local authority homes. These are sometimes referred to as 'Part III Accommodation' and admission would invariably be arranged by Social Services. If someone does not like the particular accommodation suggested, they can turn it down and ask the department what other offers might be available. Weekly charges start from about £225. However, see Financial Assistance, over.

Nursing homes

Nursing homes provide medical supervision and fully qualified nurses, 24 hours a day. Most are privately run, with the remainder supported by voluntary organisations. All nursing homes must be registered with the local Health Authority which keeps a list of what homes are available in the area.

Private. Average fees are between £350 and £500 a week, with some of the plusher nursing homes very much more expensive. For information contact: **The Registered Nursing Home Association**,

Calthorpe House, Hagley Road, Edgbaston, Birmingham B16 8QY.
T:0121 454 2511.

Voluntary organisations. Charges start around £383 a week.
Applications should be made either via Social Services or direct to the
home manager.

Financial assistance for residential and nursing home care

Under the community care arrangements people needing to go into a
residential or nursing home may receive help from their Social
Services department.

As explained earlier, the department will make the arrangements
direct with the home following their assessment procedure and will
seek reimbursement from the person towards the cost, according to set
means-testing rules.

**People who were already in a residential or nursing home before
April 1993** continue receiving special levels of Income Support as
before. The current maximum weekly amount (2001/02) for residential
care homes is between £225 and £308 (£47 higher in London); and for
nursing homes, between £337 and £379 (£52 higher in London). N.B.
This arrangement (known as 'preserved rights') is due to cease in April
2002: from then onwards the full cost of residential care will be met by
the individual's local authority.

People who had been or are currently paying for themselves but
can no longer afford to do so may have the right to claim help, now or
in the future, if they qualify on grounds of financial need – for example
if their savings fall to £18,500. People with assets below £11,500 will
not have to pay anything.

Free nursing care. As from October 2001, the nursing costs of being
in a home will be free to all patients. This does not include the personal
care costs (e.g. help with bathing, dressing or eating) nor the accommodation costs, both of which individuals will continue to be assessed
for under the present rules.

Further information

Key sources of information about voluntary and private homes are: the
Charities Digest and the *Directory of Independent Hospitals and Health
Services*. Ask at the library.

Elderly Accommodation Counsel, 3rd Floor, 89 Albert Embankment, London SE1 7TP. T:020 7820 1343. Has a nationwide database of all types of suitable accommodation to meet the needs of older people, including sheltered housing, residential care and nursing homes.

Help the Hospices, 34–44 Britannia Street, London WC1X 9JG. T:020 7520 8200. A national charity dedicated to the support of hospices for terminally ill people. Can provide a list of charitable hospices and other information.

Cinnamon Trust, Foundry House, Foundry Square, Hayle, Cornwall TR27 4HH. T:01736 757900. Maintains a register of residential and care homes that allow pets to be kept.

Social Services Departments keep lists of both voluntary and private homes.

Some special problems

A minority of people, as they become older, suffer from special problems which can cause great distress. Because families do not like to talk about them, they may be unaware of what services are available so may be missing out both on practical help and sometimes also on financial assistance.

Hypothermia

Elderly people tend to be more vulnerable to the cold. If the body drops below a certain temperature, it can be dangerous because one of the symptoms of hypothermia is that sufferers no longer actually feel cold. For this reason, during a cold snap it is very important to check up regularly on an elderly person living alone.

Insulation can play a large part in keeping a home warmer and cheaper to heat. There are various grants available to assist with this. See heating and insulation sections in Chapter 7.

Your parents might qualify for cold weather payments. See page 172.

Incontinence

Incontinence can cause deep embarrassment to sufferers as well as inconvenience to relatives. A doctor should always be consulted, as it can often be cured or at least alleviated by proper treatment. Some local authorities operate a laundry service which collects soiled linen, sometimes several times a week. The person to talk to is the Health Visitor or District Nurse (ring the Health Centre) who will be able to advise about this and other facilities.

Incontinence Information Helpline. T:020 7831 9831. Operates Monday to Friday from 9.30 a.m. to 4.30 p.m. and is staffed by nurses with a special understanding of bowel and bladder problems.

Dementia

Sometimes an elderly person can become confused, forgetful or have violent mood swings and at times be abnormally aggressive. It is important to consult a doctor as soon as possible as the cause may be due to depression, stress or even vitamin deficiency, all of which can be treated and often completely cured.

If dementia is diagnosed, it is usually a good idea to talk to the Health Visitor, as she will know about local support services and can also arrange appointments with other professionals.

Three organisations that can often give help and support are:

Alzheimer's Society for England, Wales and Northern Ireland, Gordon House, 10 Greencoat Place, London SW1P 1PH. T020 7306 0606. Helpline, open 8.30 a.m. to 6.30 p.m., Monday to Friday, T:0845 300 0336.

Alzheimer Scotland – Action on Dementia, 22 Drumsheugh Gardens, Edinburgh EH3 7RN. T:0808 808 3000 (24-hour helpline).

Mind (The Mental Health Charity), Granta House, 15–19 Broadway, London E15 4BQ. T:020 8519 2122; for Wales, **Mind Cymru**, 3rd Floor, Quebec House, Castlebridge, Cowbridge Road East, Cardiff CF1 9AB. T:029 2039 5123.

12

Wills, Benefits and Helpful Organisations

In Bali death is celebrated with glorious processions, merry-making and days of feasting. In Western society, we go to the other extreme. Many people never even get round to making a will, let alone discussing with their partner the financial and other practicalities should one of them die. Yet, as every widows' organisation would testify, a great deal of heartbreak and real financial worry could be avoided if husbands and wives were more open with each other.

Wills

Anyone who is married or over the age of 35 should make a will. At very least, this will ensure that their wishes are known and properly executed. It will also spare their family the legal complications that arise when someone dies intestate. A major problem if someone dies without leaving a will is that their partner will usually have to wait very much longer for badly needed cash. There will be no executor. Also, the individual's assets will be distributed according to a rigid formula, which may be a far cry from what he or she had intended.

Making a will

You have three choices: you can do it yourself; you can ask your bank to help you; or you can use a solicitor.

Doing it yourself

Homemade wills are not generally recommended. People often use imprecise wording, which could result in the donor's wishes being misinterpreted and could also cause delay in settling the estate.

You can buy forms from W H Smith and other stationers which, while helpful, still leave considerable margin for error.

Two witnesses are needed and an essential point to remember is that beneficiaries cannot witness a will; nor can the spouses of any beneficiaries. In certain circumstances, a will can be rendered invalid. A sensible precaution for anyone doing it themselves is to have it checked by a solicitor or by a legal expert from the CAB.

Banks

Advice on wills and the administration of estates is carried out by the trustee companies of most of the major high street banks.

The services they offer are: to provide general guidance, to act as executor and to administer the estate. They will also introduce clients to a solicitor and keep a copy of the will – plus other important documents – in their safe, to avoid the risk of their being mislaid. Additionally, banks (as solicitors) can give inheritance tax planning and other financial advice. Some banks will draw up a will for you.

Solicitors

Solicitors may offer to: draw up a will, act as executors and administer the estate and keep a copy of your will in safe keeping. If you do not know a solicitor, you can look in the 'Yellow Pages' or ask the Citizens' Advice Bureau.

Charges

These can vary enormously, depending on the size and complexity of the will. A basic will could cost from £50 or, if your affairs are more complicated, the cost could run into many hundreds of pounds. Always ask for an estimate before proceeding. Remember too that professional fees normally carry 17.5 per cent VAT.

Many solicitors charge according to the time they spend on a job, so although the actual work may not take very long, if you spend hours discussing your will, or changing it every few months, the costs can escalate very considerably. However, some solicitors will give you a fixed fee estimate, which should give you a good idea from the outset what the cost would be.

Community Legal Service Funding

Civil Legal Aid has been replaced by a new facility known as Community Legal Service Funding. Financial assistance for legal help and advice is available to certain groups of people for making a will. These include: people aged over 70; disabled people; and a parent of a disabled person whom they wish to provide for in their will. To qualify, they will need to satisfy the financial criteria. For further information enquire at your CAB or other advice centre.

Executors

You will need to appoint at least one executor. He/she can be a beneficiary under the estate, and can be a member of your family or a friend. Or, and this is generally advisable for larger estates, you could appoint your solicitor or bank.

The fees will be additional. They are not paid at the time of making the will but instead come out of the estate. Significant sums could be involved, so the advice on obtaining an estimate is, if anything, even more relevant. In certain instances, banks can be more expensive; in others, solicitors. The only way to discover is to get an estimate from each.

Banks publish a tariff of their charges. Solicitors render bills according to the time involved; so, although it is impossible for them to be precise, they should nevertheless be able to give a reasonable estimate – at least at the time of quoting. Both banks' and solicitors' fees may increase during the interval between their being appointed and fulfilling their duties as executor.

Other Points

Wills should always be kept in a safe place – and their whereabouts known.

You might find it helpful to obtain a mini-form, known as a Personal Assets Log, to give to your executor or close relatives. It is, quite simply, a four-sided leaflet with space to record the essential information: name and address of solicitor; where the will and other important documents are kept; the date of any codicils and so on. Logs should be obtainable from most solicitors.

Wills may sometimes need updating. For example: an existing will becomes invalid in the event of marriage or remarriage and should be revised. Any changes must be by codicil (for minor alterations) or by a new will, and must be properly witnessed.

If you have views about your funeral, it is sensible to write a letter to your executors explaining your wishes and to lodge it with your will. If you have any pets, you may equally wish to leave a letter filed with your will explaining what arrangements you have made for their imme-diate/long term welfare. The charity Pro Dogs provides special cards for this purpose for owners to complete, obtainable from: **Pro Dogs**, Rocky Bank, 6 New Road, Ditton, Maidstone, Kent ME20 6AD. T:01732 872222.

Money worries – and how to minimise them

Most people say that the first time they really think about death, in terms of what would happen to their family, is after the birth of their first baby. As children grow up, requirements change but key points that any family man or woman should consider are life insurance and mortgage protection relief.

Both husbands and wives should have **life insurance cover**. If either were to die, not only would their partner lose the benefit of their earnings, they would also lose the value of their services: home decorating, gardening, cooking and so forth.

Most banks and building societies urge homeowners to take out **mortgage protection schemes**. If you die, the loan is paid off automatically and the family home will not be repossessed. Banks also offer **insurance to cover any personal or other loans**. This could be a vital safeguard to avoid leaving the family with debts.

Many people worry about **funeral costs**. Burial services can vary, in different parts of the country, from about £1,390 to £3,930 or even more depending on the choice of coffin and other arrangements. Although you may hear of cheaper estimates, these are normally exclusive of disbursements which have to be made to the vicar and others.

While cremations are cheaper, prices have increased by more than 10 per cent over the past few years – with £1,255 being a rough average. But here again, costs can vary significantly according to both area and how grand, or simple, the arrangements are.

As a way of helping, some insurance companies offer savings plans to cover funeral costs and while these could be sensible, a drawback is that you are budgeting today against an unknown cost in the future.

A rather different type of scheme which overcomes the uncertainties is the pre-paid funeral plan, whereby you pay all the costs in advance, so sparing your family the worry of finding the money at the time.

One such scheme is the **Age Concern Funeral Plan**, T:0800 387718. Another is **Perfect Choice**, which is a 'bespoke' policy tailored to individual requirements, offered by: **National Association of Funeral Directors**, 618 Warwick Road, Solihull, West Midlands B91 1AA. T:0121 709 0019. Another organisation that, as well as a selection of standard plans, offers a personalised service that allows you to specify every detail including the choice of funeral director is **Golden Charter**, T:0800 833800.

While most pre-payment schemes are problem-free, there can be pitfalls – including the risk of losing your money, if the company which sold you the plan ceased trading. Advice from the OFT is to check the following points before paying: (1) whether your money will be paid into a trust administered by independent trustees (2) what fees are deducted from the investment (3) what exact expenses the plan covers and (4) if you cancel the plan, whether you can get all your money back – or only a part.

People on low incomes may qualify for a payment from the Social Fund to help with funeral costs. For details see leaflet D 49, *What To Do After A Death*, obtainable from any Social Security office. If the matter is urgent, make a point of asking for Form SF 200.

A very real crisis for some families is the need for immediate money while waiting for the estate to be settled. At least part of the problem can be overcome by couples having a **joint bank account**, with both partners having drawing rights without the signature of the other being required. Sole-name bank accounts and joint accounts requiring both signatures are frozen.

For the same reason, it may also be a good idea for any savings or investments to be held in the joint name of the couple.

An essential practical point for all couples is that any financial and **other important documents should be discussed together**. Even today, an all too common saga is for widows to come across insurance policies and other papers, which they have never seen before and do not understand – often causing quite unnecessary anxiety. A further common-sense 'must' is for both partners to **know where important papers are kept**. Best idea is either to lock them, filed together, in a home safe; or to give them to the bank for safe keeping.

If someone dies, **the bank manager should be notified as soon as possible**, so he can assist with the problems of unpaid bills and help work out a solution until the estate is settled. The same goes for the **suppliers of essential services**: gas, electricity, telephone and so on. Unless they know the situation, there is a risk of services being cut off if there is a delay in paying the bill. Add too any credit card companies, where if bills lie neglected, the additional interest could mount up alarmingly.

Useful reading

What To Do After A Death. Free booklet from Social Security offices.

Arranging A Funeral, free factsheet from Age Concern, Freepost (SWB 30375), Ashburton, Devon TQ13 7ZZ; or telephone free T:0800 009966. A separate Scottish version is available.

State benefits, tax and other money points

Several extra financial benefits are given to widowed persons. Most take the form of a cash payment. However, there are one or two tax and other points that it may be useful to know.

Benefits paid in cash form

There are three important cash benefits to which widowed people may be entitled: bereavement benefit, bereavement allowance and widowed parent's allowance. These have replaced the former widows' benefits, as all benefits are now payable on equal terms to men and women alike.

To claim the benefits, fill in Form BB 1, obtainable from any Social Security office. You will also be given a questionnaire (BD 8) by the Registrar. It is important that you complete this, as it acts as a trigger to speed up payment of your benefits. For more information, see leaflet NP 45 *A Guide to Bereavement Benefits*.

Bereavement benefit. This has replaced what used to be known as widow's payment. It is a tax-free lump sum of £2,000, paid as soon as an individual is widowed provided that: (1) their spouse had paid sufficient NI contributions (2) they personally are under State retirement age or (3) if over State retirement age, their husband/wife had not been entitled to retirement pension.

Bereavement allowance. This has replaced the widow's pension. Women already in receipt of widow's pension before 6 April 2001 are not affected and will continue to receive their widow's pension as normal.

The new bereavement allowance is for those aged between 45 and State pension age who do not receive widowed parent's allowance. It is payable for 52 weeks. As with widow's pension before, there are various levels of payment: the full rate and age-related bereavement allowance. Receipt in all cases is dependent on sufficient NI contributions having been paid.

Full-rate bereavement allowance is paid to widowed persons between the ages of 55 and 59 inclusive. The weekly amount is £72.50, which is the same as the current pension for a single person.

Age-related bereavement allowance is for younger widows/widowers, who do not qualify for the full rate. It is payable to those who are aged between 45 and 54 inclusive when their partner dies. Rates depend on age and vary from £21.75 for 45 year olds to £67.43 for those aged 54.

Bereavement allowance is normally paid automatically once you have sent off your completed form BB 1, so if for any reason you do not receive it you should enquire at your local Social Security office. In the event of your being ineligible, due to insufficient NI contributions having been paid, you may still be entitled to receive income support, housing benefit or a grant or loan from the social fund. Your Social Security office will advise you.

Widowed parent's allowance. This is paid to widowed parents with at least one child for whom they receive child benefit. The current value (2001/02) is £72.50 a week. The allowance is usually paid automatically. If for some reason, although eligible, you do not receive the money, you should inform your local Social Security office. See leaflet NP 45.

Retirement pension. Once a widowed person reaches State retirement age, they should receive a State pension in the normal way. An important point to remember is that a widow/widower may be able to use their late spouse's NI contributions to boost the amount they receive. See leaflets NP 46 *A Guide to Retirement Pensions*, RM1 *Retirement*, RM2 *Approaching Retirement?* and RM3 *Retired*.

Problems. As you probably know, both pension payments and bereavement benefits are dependent on sufficient NI contributions having been paid. Your Social Security office will inform you if you are not eligible. If this should turn out to be the case, you may still be entitled to receive income support, housing benefit, council tax benefit or a grant or loan from the Social Fund – so ask. If you are unsure of your position or have difficulties, ask at your Citizens' Advice Bureau who will at least be able to help you work out the sums and inform you of your rights.

Particular points to note

- Most widowed persons' benefits are taxable. However, the £2,000 bereavement benefit is tax-free, as are pensions paid to the widow/widowers of Armed Forces personnel.
- Widowed persons will normally be able to inherit their spouse's additional pension rights, if he/she contributed to SERPS (see N.B. below); or at least half their guaranteed minimum pension, if they were in a contracted-out scheme. Additionally, where applicable, all widowed persons are entitled on retirement to half the graduated pension earned by their husband/wife.

N.B. SERPS benefits paid to surviving spouses are due to be halved over the coming years. The cuts are gradually being phased in between October 2002 and October 2010. Anyone over State pension age before 6 October 2002 will be exempt from any cuts and will keep the right to pass on their SERPS pension in full to a bereaved spouse. Equally, any younger widow or widower who had already inherited their late spouse's SERPS entitlement before 6 October 2002 will not be affected and will continue to receive the full amount.

■ Women in receipt of widow's pension who remarry, or live with a man as his wife, lose their entitlement to the payment unless, that is, the cohabitation ends in which case they can claim it again. If aged over 60, the fact that a woman may be living with a man will not affect her entitlement to a retirement pension based on her late husband's contribution record.

■ Thanks to a recent change in the law, widows/widowers of Armed Forces personnel whose deaths were a direct result of their service are now entitled to keep their Armed Forces attributable pension for life, regardless of whether they remarry or cohabit.

Tax allowances

At time of writing, widows and widowers receive the normal single person's tax allowance of £4,535 a year and, if in receipt of married couple's allowance, are also entitled to any unused portion of the allowance in the year of their partner's death. Those aged 65 and older may be entitled to a higher personal allowance, (see page 47).

Useful Inland Revenue leaflets. These are available from any tax office.

IR 45: *What to do About Tax When Someone Dies*
IR 90: *Tax Allowances and Reliefs*
IHT 3: *An Introduction to Inheritance Tax.*

Advice. Many people have difficulty in working out exactly what they are entitled to – and how to claim it. The Citizens' Advice Bureau is always very helpful; as are Cruse and the National Association of Widows (see below).

Organisations that can help

Problems vary. For some, the hardest thing to bear is the loneliness of returning to an empty house. For others, money problems seem to dominate everything else. For many older women in particular, who have not got a job, widowhood creates a great gulf where for a while there is no real sense of purpose. Many widowed men and women go through a spell of feeling enraged against their partner for dying.

Most are baffled and hurt by the seeming indifference of friends, who appear more embarrassed than sympathetic.

In time, all these feelings soften, problems diminish and individuals are able to recapture their joy for living with all its many pleasures. Talking to other people who know the difficulties from their own experience can be a tremendous help. The following organisations not only offer opportunities for companionship but also provide an advisory and support service.

Cruse Bereavement Care, Cruse House, 126 Sheen Road, Richmond, Surrey TW9 1UR. Helpline T:0870 167 1677 (9.30 a.m. – 5.30 p.m.). Offers free help, advice and counselling through its 178 local branches to anyone who has been bereaved. There are drop-in centres and friendship groups plus a list of publications. For further information, contact your local branch (see telephone directory) or the address above.

National Association of Widows, 48 Queen's Road, Coventry CV1 3EH. T:024 7663 4848. The Association is a national voluntary organisation. Its many branches provide a supportive social network for widows throughout the country. Membership is £7.50 a year.

Many professional and other groups offer a range of services for widows and widowers associated with them. Trade unions are often particularly supportive, as are Rotary Clubs, all the armed forces organisations and most benevolent societies. Many local Age Concern groups offer a counselling service.

Index